THEN · AGAIN

How to Write the Story of Your Life

Including Real Examples and Practical Exercises

by

Carla Rich Montez

Printed by CreateSpace, An Amazon.com Company
ISBN -13: 978-0-692-09815-8

This is a work of nonfiction. All quotes, stories, and images are used by permission of the authors or their designees.

Cover design and book layout by Janie Kelley.

*This book is dedicated
to the participants in my life story writing program.
Because you have shared your memories,
generations will know you,
and in that, they will know themselves.*

With Gratitude To...

Janie – for designing Then · Again.
You made this book both beautiful and engaging;

Kate – for your wise counsel, for your faith in me,
and for recognizing that this book was necessary;

Mary – for immediately supporting this book
when it was only an idea;

Merrill – for being such a dedicated co-teacher,
masterful life story writer, and genuinely good man;

Mom and Dad – for telling me I could be anything I wanted to be.
You really made this book possible;

My kids –
Katie – for your unfailing interest in me
and your loving encouragement of this project;

Chris – for your commitment to excellence and positive attitude.
You inspired me many times during this project;

John – for being such good company especially on writing days.
I was never the lonely writer because you were always near;

Nancy – for inviting me to co-teach a class about memoir writing
and for suggesting to Merrell that he do the same;

Steve – for lattes and scones and for your unceasing support
of my life story writing program;

Sue – for vigorous editing that remarkably improved the manuscript.
In that process, you made me a better writer;

And *Tess, Bailey, Emmy, and Idgie* – for your constant companionship,
you good dogs.

I would also like to recognize Bradley University and its lifelong
learning institutes which allowed me to provide life story writing
workshops in the community.

Preface

The single purpose of this book
is to help you write the story of your life.

CONTENTS

The following writers generously provided memories
from their own life stories so that you could see
how the techniques in *Then·Again* can lead to real results.
Their stories are sure to inspire you!

Contributors

Contributors

HOW TO WRITE THE STORY
OF YOUR LIFE

CHAPTER 1

"*I come from a long line
of story tellers,
but no one
wrote them down.
I'm trying to break
that pattern.*"

\- Judith Michael Sowers

How many of you have a picture like this?

How many of you have a picture like this, and you don't know who it is?

I have "mystery" photos too. In fact, I have lots of them. They're all stored in a cardboard box in the back of one of my closets because I don't know what to do with them. On one hand, I should keep them because they might be pictures of relatives. On the other hand, I will probably never know who they are, so maybe I should just donate them to the local historical society.

Between these episodes of equivocation, I occasionally look at a picture—like this one—and I study it for clues that might connect the individual to me.

That cautious smile resembles the one of my stoic grandmother.
Are they related?

She's wearing a pearl necklace that looks like one my mother wore.
Could it be the same one?

Her hair is wavy and even a little unruly
—just like most of the people on my dad's side of the family.

One of her eyes is slightly askew.
I have a cousin who has a droopy eye like that.

3

Of course, this is all speculation, and I remain unable to identify this woman. But I keep her picture—in that box in the back of the closet—*just in case.*

This is an all-too-familiar condition isn't it—that we have old photos of people we can't identify? And aren't we all a little bit saddened when those pictures are the only record we have of those people?

So here's a proposition. Let's make sure that we don't allow this to happen to ourselves. Let's leave a legacy more meaningful than a collection of mysterious old photographs.

In the timeline of our family history, let's make sure there's not a gap in the story line.

Let's write the story of your life.

THEN · AGAIN

CHAPTER 2

"*This is the answer
to a wish I have had
for a long time—
—to have guidance
in writing about
my life.*"

- Anonymous
from a 2012 workshop evaluation

The first thing I want you to know is that you're not alone if you feel challenged by the prospect of writing your life story. Aspiring life story writers everywhere share many of the same concerns you do:

You're getting some pressure. Family members are asking you to write down the stories you've been telling them over the years.

You're getting older. You're beginning to realize that you're at *that* age when you need to start documenting some of your experiences.

You're skeptical. *My life covers a lot of years. It's not possible to write about everything I've ever done.*

You're concerned. *I'm not a good writer. I can't do this.*

You're busy. *I've got a lot of things on my plate right now. I'll get to it eventually.*

The result of all these misgivings is that you haven't written your life story yet.

Or you've started. And stopped. And started again.

So the story of your life is still swimming around in your head. You have this collection of memories that you want to record; you have friends and family encouraging you; but you're stuck.

Now what?

My guess is that you're ready to try something different, and so I say, "Welcome! You're in the right place!" In this book, we're going to work together to address your challenges so that you can finally start writing your life story, keep writing, and enjoy recalling every page of it.

How will we approach this project? For one thing, we're going to focus on your inborn ability to tell a story. That means we're not going to concern ourselves with grammar and construction. Instead, we'll talk about staying true to the natural way you express yourself.

We're also going to celebrate the ordinary. Rather than writing about only the apex events of your life, we're going to also find memories in your day-to-day living. Be prepared to discover the unexpected pleasure of writing about the familiar.

Next, we'll talk about ways to remember, so you can always have a ready source of story ideas. You will be glad to know that memories are all around you, so noticing them will be our quest. If you can do this, you'll never have to look at a blank sheet of paper and wonder what to write.

Along the way, we'll learn how to organize your stories and turn them into a collection for sharing with family and friends, and we'll talk about strategies you can use to sustain the momentum you've started here.

By the way, we're not going to just talk about writing, we're going to *do* some writing. So you'll find many exercises throughout the book. But don't worry! You won't have to take any tests. These assignments are simply a way to help you take concrete steps to start writing—and keep writing—your life story. As a bonus feature, we will also connect exercises to real examples so that you can *See How It's Done.*

If you have some questions, you'll enjoy the FAQs section where we'll talk about some of the issues that many life story writers share. And if you're a practicing or aspiring teacher, I've created a chapter just for you, *Ideas for Teachers*, my suggestions for creating your own life story writing program.

Best of all, you're going to read examples of *real* life stories. In Section 2, you'll find stories written by people who have participated in my workshops and who have generously offered to share their stories with you. Their work is sure to inspire you. And here's a bonus: be prepared to start reminiscing. Their memories will trigger yours, so make sure you have a notebook nearby when you read their stories.

As a beginning life story writer, you may not yet realize that a lot of people want you to succeed. Many of them are your family and friends. Some of them are people you have never met. But all of us want to encourage you. So think of this book as your personal cheering squad. Go, You!

Now, let's get started.

ASSIGNMENT

Find an old photograph that holds good memories for you. Maybe you have a special picture from your vacation last year, or you've kept a photo of the house you grew up in.

Once you've found a picture, tell someone about it. Sit down with your spouse or your sibling or a good friend, and talk to that person about your photograph.

When was it taken? What are the memories you associate with the photo?

What's the story that goes with your picture?

CHAPTER 3

"I have been so afraid
that I am not a great writer
or even a good writer,
but I think that I can begin
to let that go."

— Belevia Gibson

Have you ever told a story?

That may seem like an absurd question, but it's an important one for you to consider in the context of writing your life story.

Of course, the answer is yes. Each of us has told a story—about what happened at work today, or what we did on vacation last summer, or what the guys talked about at the barbershop on Saturday. I would even go so far to say that most of us are *accomplished* in the art of story-telling because we do it nearly every single day.

Isn't that what you did when you talked about your picture? Didn't you *tell* a story about it?

My theory, then, is that you already command the signature skill of the life story writer. You can tell a story.

What may be holding you back, then, is the other skill you need—to be able to write. While you may be good at telling a story, you're not as confident that you can write one.

I suspect some of the reason you feel that way is that you have been conditioned to think that writing has to be perfect—that it must be grammatically correct and properly constructed for it to be effective. Who among us doesn't have the memory of a composition generously inked in red for all its "bad" writing? And who of us doesn't wince at the prospect of being judged for our writing skills?

One of the unfortunate outcomes of this focus on writing technique is that is can frustrate the life story writer who simply wants to tell a story with written words. Instead, we work so hard at writing correctly that we lose track of our own voice. In the interest of "good" writing, we remove all the nuances and idiosyncrasies and colloquialisms of our spoken language until our written stories no longer sound like us *at all*.

Where is the pleasure in that? And how many unfinished life stories are hidden in desk drawers because of such frustrations?

If you have put your life story on the back burner because you're worried about your writing skills, let me offer this encouragement. Your writing is perfect—as is. Whether your writing is classically constructed or full of the quirky expressions you're known for, it sounds just like you. Isn't that what you want—to be *heard* in your own story?

Or think about it this way, if you were to find a journal that was written by your mother, what would matter more: how *well* she wrote, or *that* she wrote?

ASSIGNMENT

Using the photograph that you talked about in the last chapter, write 2-3 pages about its memories. Don't worry about grammar and construction. Just *tell* the story—in writing.

~

SEE HOW IT'S DONE

As you read some of the stories in Section 2, look for writing styles that "sound" good to you—that make you feel like the writer is talking. Look for a style that is comfortable, casual, or that seems unconstrained by writing conventions.

THEN · AGAIN

CHAPTER 4

"One story
triggered another,
an unexpected and
serendipitous bonus
to the writing process."

- Laurie Hartshorn

Before we go any farther, let's make sure we share the same vocabulary. What is a life story, and what's the process for writing one?

I view the life story as a collection of stories written about individual memories. Most of the time, these stories are complete in themselves. Each has a beginning, middle, and end and recounts a single event or memory. In fact, you experienced writing about a single memory when you wrote a story about your photograph.

Eventually, these individual stories accumulate and are then compiled into a form, typically a book (although some writers may choose to create electronic versions of their stories—more on this in Chapter 11). Regardless of its final form, the result of all your writing is that *the life story is a collection of life stories.*

When you first begin writing your life story, you may wonder how you will organize it. Where will your life story begin? And how will it flow from one story to the next?

One way to structure your life story is to write your memories in chronological order. Writers who choose this approach may begin their stories with their earliest childhood memories and continue their writing, in calendar order, until they reach the events of the present day.

A variation of writing in chronological order is to begin from an arbitrary starting point. For example, your story could start with your wedding day followed by memories highlighting each year of marriage. Similarly, you might choose to focus on your military career beginning with your induction and concluding with your last day of service.

The advantage of writing your memories chronologically is that your writing plan is prescribed. You can sit down every day with the assurance of knowing what story you're going to write, because your writing will be sequenced by a timeline.

You may also be tested by this plan when you realize that your writing will cover a long span of time. Five years? Forty years? That's a lot of time to document, a lot of stories to write. The perceived scope of such a project may be overwhelming.

So, if you decide to write your stories in chronological order, think about ways you can manage the volume. For example, instead of writing stories about *every* grade in school, write about the highlights of school, in general. Rather than writing stories about every job you've held, write instead about the ones that most impacted you. When you can "chunk" your life into eras like this, you will be adjusting the scope of your writing to a more manageable volume.

Another way to structure your life story is to write your stories in random order. Writers who choose this strategy allow their memories to guide the sequence of their writing. In other words, stories are recounted as *the memories come back to you.*

Let's look an example of how this approach could play out if your writing day began with a memory of a football game you recently attended at your alma mater.

> Writing about that game might remind you of the friends who routinely tailgated with you while you were in college. Memories of your friends may remind you of your wedding day which those friends attended. Your wedding day may remind you of your own daughter's upcoming marriage. And she may remind you that you'll soon be taking care of her dog while she's away on business. And her dog will stir memories of the retriever who was your constant companion as a child.

Five stories (or more) could come from that string of memories, yet those memories will have returned to you completely out of date order. If you follow their lead, you will be allowing your memories to determine the sequence of your writing.

The challenge of the writing-follows-memories approach is that it may feel completely haphazard. Thus, it may be an uncomfortable style for the writer who likes a predictable structure.

Fortunately, order eventually comes when all the stories are complete. Viewed in total, your stories will suggest themes, and those themes will present some sequencing ideas that will help you organize your book

For example, if you wrote several stories that were triggered by the memories that unfolded at the football game, you could organize them this way. One group of stories might consist of college memories. Another may suggest a chapter about meeting your spouse. A third group may center on memories about parenting. And a fourth may consist of dog stories. By examining your stories *collectively*, you'll find structure.

One of the advantages of the writing-follows-memories approach is that the writing is more intuitive because it follows your train of thought. You simply write about the memory that's right in front of you, and this removes the pressure to follow a pre-planned list of story ideas. Some describe their writing as less forced, or even effortless. It just—flows.

So the next step is for you to write about some memories, and then decide which sequencing style is more comfortable to you. Will you prefer to write your stories in chronological order, or will it be more natural for you to recount your memories as they come back to you? Before you decide, try both styles.

In no time at all, you'll realize that one style suits you better than the other. When this happens, you will have found the approach that will help sustain your writing long term—until you eventually complete your life story.

ASSIGNMENT

Imagine that you are working on your life story, and you're trying to decide how to organize your writing. Which style will most suit the way you like to write? Do you think you will prefer the structure offered by writing your memories in chronological order? Or will you choose the "no structure" approach in which your writing follows your memories?

Can you think of other ways that you can order your writing? Maybe you prefer to start with the present and work backwards. Or perhaps you want to write only about a single era, like stories focused on your career life.

Which approach feels more comfortable to you? Which one will be so satisfying that you will continue your writing?

~

SEE HOW IT'S DONE

Some of the stories in Section 2 are written as individual events while others are part of a sequence of events. In other words, you may read stories that stand alone while others feel like they're part of a series. As you notice these distinctions, think about the way you want to sequence your own writing. Will your writing follow your memories, or will it follow a timeline?

THEN · AGAIN

CHAPTER 5

"Stories don't have to be
about major events.
All of us can write stories
about ordinary,
everyday memories."

- Kathy Carter

Sometimes, people put off writing their life stories because they believe they don't have anything special to say, that they're just ordinary. Have you ever felt that way?

I wonder if my grandma had similar feelings. She was a typical farm wife of the early 20th century, so like most of her peers, she had a diverse set of responsibilities. These duties included typical household tasks like cooking, ironing, and cleaning. But they also included jobs like carrying buckets of water from the well to the house, starting a wood fire in the stove, taking care of livestock, maintaining a large garden, making the family linens and clothing, and preserving food. All of these chores were accomplished without the benefit of electricity, running water, or other modern conveniences.

Because every farm wife did what Grandma did, her life was pretty ordinary by the standards of the day. And so it didn't really occur to her that she was doing anything out-of-the ordinary. That acceptance probably explains why she never wrote any stories about her life.

But her life's circumstances suggest that she experienced conditions very different from ours. And consequently, we would all have questions for her about how she managed. What was it like to cook on a wood-burning stove? Was it tiring to use a treadle sewing machine? How did she endure the weight of a flat-iron to remove wrinkles from all the clothes?

And what was it like to do the laundry this way?

Grandma's laundry day began when she pumped water out of the well. Once the buckets were full, she brought them into the house, put wood in the stove, started a fire, and heated the water. When it was hot enough, she poured the water into a barrel-shaped wooden tub, scrubbed the clothes on a galvanized washboard (using soap she had made on another day), rinsed the clothes in a second tub of water, squeezed the water out by running the clothes through a hand-cranked wringer, and then hauled all the damp clean clothes outdoors to hang them on the clothesline. In the winter, the process began with heating the house before heating the water. And since the clothes were still hung outdoors, garments froze to the line and had to be pried from it when they were (mostly) dry. They were then stacked like boards to bring back into the house where they thawed and finished drying.

Given these conditions, wouldn't you like to read Grandma's account of laundry day, or any of her other *routine* chores?

And if we could read those stories, do you think we would believe that she led an *ordinary* life?

In fact, had she written, Grandma's stories could teach us some things.

For instance, her stories might contribute to our understanding of history. Through her eyes, we might be able to discover how common household tools were used, or perhaps we would develop some new understanding of the physiology of early 20th century farm women.

Her memories might also shed some light on our cultural past. While Grandma's laundry practices began with a washboard in a wooden tub, they evolved to include a motorized washing machine and dryer. In that same span of time, she also watched Neil Armstrong walk on the moon when her own transportation story began with a horse and buggy. What could Grandma's stories teach us about adapting to change or human resilience?

Grandma's stories might also provide her with her own insights. What would she notice about her life as she relived it? What reflection might she have in looking back? And what new ground might she yet want to explore in her writing?

As for me, Grandma's story would be a precious find. Through her memories, I would learn a lot about her—not only about her chores but also about her thinking and her concerns—what is was like *to be her*. Maybe I would even recognize some traits connecting her to me.

And that connection is why *your* ordinary life is worth writing about. Not only does it have value to our history, to our culture, and to our families, your ordinariness is an essential component of understanding your *self*.

So please remember that life stories are not reserved just for the famous or for mountaintop experiences. Every person and subject has worth. And every story has a deeper message.

Sometimes, our stories even teach us something about ourselves.

ASSIGNMENT

Let's celebrate the ordinary! Write a 2- or 3-page story about a meal you remember—not just the menu but also the details surrounding it.

~

SEE HOW IT'S DONE

What do you notice about the topics of the stories in Section 2? Which stories seem to best capture routine, everyday moments in our lives? What "ordinary" events in your life are worthy of a story?

CHAPTER 6

"*Often, without realizing it,*
I am reminded
of an event or experience
by a smell or a sound
associated with the past."

- John McNally

Have you ever found yourself struggling to remember something —you can't recall a name, or you don't know where you left your keys? Have you walked into a room and wondered, "Why did I come in here?"

Memory challenges like these impact all of us—and more so as we get older. And even though these lapses are fleeting, they're still frustrating, maybe even disconcerting. They can make us feel like we're losing our mind—or our memory.

If you've ever felt this way, then it's possible that you might also be contemplating whether you're up to the task of writing your life story.

Will I be able to remember an event from forty years ago, when I can't even recall what day it is?

First, let me offer some assurance. You haven't lost your mind, and your memories are still intact. The *real* problem is that you are distracted.

Frankly, we are *all* distracted at one time or another, so we don't pay attention to what we're *supposed* to be doing. Instead, our thoughts get our attention. We allow the chatter in our brains to divert our thinking. It's in those moments of absent-mindedness that we put down our keys—and then can't remember where we left them.

For life story writers, the loss of concentration can be especially risky because it allows thoughts to get in the way of our memories. In other words, a distracted mind isn't really effective at reminiscing because it's just too busy processing other, mostly irrelevant, information.

Luckily our memories aren't so easily dissuaded. They *want* to be noticed, so they resort to a clever tactic. They come back to us through our senses.

We're all familiar with this process. It's what you experience whenever a certain smell or taste brings back a memory. In the same way that the scent of cinnamon reminds you of your grandmother's rolls, our senses help us remember.

Thus the senses serve as subtle attention-getters. They cut through the babbling in our minds, and they send us a memory. When this happens, we realize we *can* remember.

So you're not losing your mind, and you haven't forgotten your past. Your memories are all around you—in the things you see, hear, smell, taste, and touch. Your challenge, then, is simply to quiet your mind and pay attention.

Here's an exercise to help you.

ASSIGNMENT

Find a place outdoors that you really enjoy. This place can be in a park or on your patio or any place where you can appreciate the outdoors.

Now sit down, close your eyes, and get quiet. Let go of your thoughts, and begin to clear your mind of all its distractions. (By the way, this may not happen quickly. It takes practice to still your mind. Don't give up!)

With your eyes still closed and your mind quieted, pay attention to what you hear. Listen to all the sounds that are around you—those nearby and those in the distance; those above you and below you. Notice even the subtle vibrations that may crop up.

While you're concentrating on all the sounds around you, try to suppress the other senses, so that you focus only on what you hear. Simply sit, and listen.

When you're finished, think about these questions: How did it feel to still your thoughts? When you were quiet, did you hear anything new — things that may have always been there but that you had not noticed before? Did a certain sound remind you of something from your past?

~

SEE HOW IT'S DONE

Read the stories in Section 2, and see if you can identify the memories that were triggered by a sense. Try to imagine how you can use your senses to help you remember.

CHAPTER 7

"The smell of carnations
always reminds me
of my first prom
and the corsage
I had pinned on me."

- Susan S.

I believe so deeply that the senses are doorways to our memories that I want them to do their magic with you. So in this chapter, we're going to return to our outdoor place several more times to singularly explore a sense. Each time, we will still our minds, pay attention, and then we will write about the memories that are triggered by our sensory observations.

Take a notebook with you. You'll want to keep track of all the stories that come back to you!

ASSIGNMENT

Return to your outdoor place. Now sit down, close your eyes, and pay attention to what you **smell**. Face the wind to capture the aromas and fragrances that it carries. Notice both good and bad smells. What captures your attention, and what does it remind you of?

ASSIGNMENT

In a few days, visit your outdoor place again. This time, focus on what you **see**. Look in all directions—even up and down—and observe the different sizes, shapes, colors, and textures that are in your field of vision. Notice foreground and background; darkness and light. Look for the memories in what you see.

ASSIGNMENT

At your outdoor place, today you are going to pay attention through your sense of **touch**. You have many receptors for this sense. Your hands, feet, skin, tongue, and lips each have ways of experiencing touch, so use each of them as you make your observations. Temperature and texture also have sensations, so be aware they add a dimension to your observations. And some touches are unpleasant, like mosquito bites or injuries. What memories come back to you through all these touch channels?

ASSIGNMENT

When it's time to pay attention through **taste**, you may want to make sure there is something you can put in your mouth. Perhaps this is food, but there are non-food tastes too—for example, medicine, grass, or snow. Also consider all your taste receptors—your tongue, lips, and taste buds. And notice that texture and temperature offer additional insights. As you taste, look for a memory. What stories do you recall that are associated with a taste?

~

SEE HOW IT'S DONE

While many of the stories in Section 2 were triggered by a sense, some of the writers used the senses to trigger their memories. In other words, a memory was recreated by asking questions like, what smell do I most remember? What memory do I have about a favorite taste? Can you think of a memory that can be recalled through each of your senses?

CHAPTER 8

*"I find myself pausing
as I write
to reflect back and
call to mind the scene,
as it was then,
in order to find
those extra details
that fill the scene
and make it come to life."*

- Sue N.

As you gain more experience paying attention, you'll begin to realize that the quality of your writing is maturing. You'll spend more time finding the right word, or you'll become thoughtful about the way you describe something. These are indicators that you are becoming more observant and that you want your writing to be more engaging.

In practice, life stories *should* be more than a bland accounting of facts because our memories are full of details. In fact, if you look at the meal story you wrote in an earlier chapter, you will probably discover that you can add fine points that will make it more interesting.

So let's do some editing.

ASSIGNMENT

Go back to your meal story, and reconstruct it in your mind. Use your senses to parse the elements of the day to help you find details that you may have originally overlooked. What were the sounds that you heard at that meal—conversations, laughter, kitchen noises? Describe the scene—the table and chairs, the linens, the dishes, the lighting. Who was at the meal, where did they sit, what did they wear, and what did they do or talk about? Describe the tastes you most recall. What were the smells? How would you describe the food and its varied textures, flavors, and smells. Do you recall hugs, handshakes, or other physical contact?

~

SEE HOW IT'S DONE

Study the meal stories in Section 2. What do you notice about the details? How is your writing impacted when you recreate your memories through the filters of what you see, hear, smell, taste, and touch?

Once you start adding details, you'll notice that your writing is becoming more gratifying. As you re-construct an event, you will be able to add details that may have originally escaped you. Dishes that once featured a floral trim will become ivory colored china bearing a pink and green three-petal fleur-de-lis pattern. Details like these will not only enliven your writing, they'll also provide some reassurance.

I remember so much more than I realize.

And don't overlook the impact on your readers. Fifty years from now, your story's details will offer a next-best-thing-to-being-there experience, and this can have an emotional effect—especially on your relatives. Through your writing, you will have given them the gift of experiencing your life through your eyes (and all your other senses).

CHAPTER 9

"*I have more
to write about
than I thought.*"

- Dottie Strickler

So far, we have discussed many of the challenges that face life story writers—how to write, what to write, and how to remember. In the chapters that follow, we will talk about organizing your stories into a finished product and strategies for sustaining your writing.

Right now, though, it's time to practice. So I'd like for you to write some stories. Using what you've learned so far, go find a memory, and write about it.

But just in case you need some inspiration, here are a few subjects to trigger some memories.

ASSIGNMENT

Looking at the list below, see if you find a topic that you connect to a memory. What story do you associate with any of these items?

Prom	Pedal pushers	78 records
Radio programs	Bedtime stories	Pet
Favorite teacher	Ration stamps	Skate key
Milk man, Ice man	Sock hop	Party line
Playing in the band	Green Stamps	Sledding
Drive-in movies	Shucking gloves	Watergate
Model T	Red Rover	Penny loafers
Route 66	War	Kennedy assassination
The twist	Leisure suit	Hope chest
Black-and-white television	Campfire	Woodstock
Red hots	Burning leaves	8-track tape
	Soda fountain	Rotary phone

~

SEE HOW IT'S DONE

Read the stories in Section 2, and make a list of the topics they include. What memories do they trigger for your future writing? Can you think of other steps you can take to help you remember your past?

---

CHAPTER 10

*"Writing about
my own life
and experiences
helps me realize
where I have been
and what
I have become."*

- Jim Feurer

Eventually you will write enough stories that a book will begin to take shape. Whether it's ten pages or a hundred, your life story will be a more polished and cohesive piece if you add a few final touches. Here are some suggestions for you.

First, identify the pages you still need to write that typically open and close a book. For instance:

- What does the title page look like?
- Does your book have a table of contents?
- Will your life story have a dedication or acknowledgements page?
- Does your book need an introduction or preface to set the stage or tone?
- Will it need an index for finding keywords, people, or topics?
- Will you have an appendix that supplements your stories, for example a diagram of your family tree or a copy of your birth certificate?
- Would you like to incorporate mementos like photographs, letters, or other memorabilia?
- If your book is a gift, will it include a blank page on which you can write a personal message?

Next, think about the continuity of your book. How will your writing transition from story to story or chapter to chapter? Should your book include chapter or section titles to help it flow? What additional writing can you do to help unify the stories?

Finally, give some thought to the last chapter. What sentiments do you want to convey at the end of your book? How will you tie everything together? Consider addressing questions like these:

- What are the lessons I learned or the mistakes I made?
- What do I most value? What matters?
- What is my purpose? Why am I here?

- How would I like to be remembered?
- What advice would I give my younger self, or the reader?
- If I had it to do all over again, what would I do differently?
- How have I changed over time?
- What were some of the turning points?

ASSIGNMENT

Now that you have written several stories, start thinking about the features you can add to your book that will make it a fully rounded piece. What elements do you want to add to the beginning and ending? What can you do to help your chapters transition from one to another? What insights do you want to share in your last chapter?

THEN · AGAIN

CHAPTER 11

*"It seems to me
it would be a great shame
if anyone thinks
these stories
have to be left
on a shelf
... or stashed away
to be discovered
when we're
dead and gone."*

- D.L. Smith

In this chapter, we're going to talk about the final product—the physical expression of your book. Decisions you make about it now will impact its appearance, longevity, and cost, so let's discuss some of the options that you will want to consider.

Let's start by imagining your finished life story. What does it look like when you hold it in your hands? Is it a leather-bound volume or a flash drive? Is it something you page through, or do you look at it on a computer screen? Will you print ten copies of it or upload it to the web? In other words, is your final product a printed book or an electronic book (e-book)?

If you decide that your life story is going to be a printed book, you will need to think about the materials you'll choose.

- What kind of cover do you visualize? Options range from leather to card stock; from paper to plastic.
- How will your book be bound? You can choose from formal options like stitching or adhesives or more conventional choices such as three-ring binders or staples.
- What can you do to preserve your book so that it will last a long time? Learn about paper and ink choices, and become informed about the dangers of using items that can degrade paper such as tape, paper clips, and plastics.

If you decide that your life story is going to be an e-book, it will exist in some digital form, not on paper. Naturally, this will involve a different set of considerations such as:

- Where will your e-book be stored? On a flash drive, CD, or website? Or will it live in the cloud?
- What platform will it use? Will it be a word processing document, PDF, HTML file, or some other electronic form?
- Will your e-book include recordings or images? And how will you handle links to websites, images, or files?

- Will you ever want a paper copy of your e-book? If so, how can you adapt your files for printing?

*Regardless of your book's final form—whether printed or electronic—*it will be a more attractive and legible piece if it has a good layout. That means you'll need to make decisions about features like margins and spacing. You'll also want to choose which font you will use and what size it will be. Together, these elements will make your book more readable.

You may also want your book to incorporate creative features like borders and shading, or maybe more elaborate artwork like images or graphics. And don't forget that all these considerations apply to the front and back covers where design and layout are also required.

As you may have concluded, there are many factors to consider, and this is only a partial list of the many decisions you will make about your final product. So let this chapter serve as a starting point for conversations with the experts. Artists and graphic designers can offer advice on layout; printers and bindery professionals can help you determine how to hold your book together; archivists can advise you about preservation; and digital specialists can help you configure your electronic files.

As you are sorting through all the options available to you, never lose track of the significance of your work. Keep in mind that your life story is a once-in-a-lifetime project of extraordinary personal value. It is eminently worthy of the investment you will make in its appearance and longevity.

ASSIGNMENT

What form will your life story take? To help you answer this question, take this chapter with you, and use it to consult with the experts. Ask them to help guide you through all the options so that your final product is attractive, affordable, and exactly what you envision.

CHAPTER 12

"My [life story] writing has become a part of my life."

- Anonymous
from a 2014 workshop evaluation

When my writing workshop comes to an end, the participants are sorry that it's over.

It's not because I'm an exceptional teacher (though I'm trying.)

And it's not because people will miss the cookies we provide (which are THE BEST.)

The participants are sorry the workshop is over because they have spent the last six weeks sharing their lives with each other. In that process, they've disclosed very personal stories, they've encouraged each other, and they've collectively figured out ways to get their memories out of their heads and onto a piece of paper. The result is that they have become a community of confidants, collaborators, and friends.

So when they're sorry the workshop is about to end, they're not sorry that the writing will end (though the writing really matters to them). They're sorry they won't be together.

That's when I remind them that it's the writing that binds them, and it's the writing that so satisfies them. All this goodness exists *because* they write.

So writing matters. It's important and gratifying work, and it's worthy of our commitment to do it with some intentionality. But what does "purposeful" writing look like? What can writers do to ensure that their writing has some prominence in their lives?

First, embrace your purpose. Be proud that your writing is about your life. It is the most original and authentic writing you will ever do, and no one on earth can do it as well as you.

Second, make time for your writing. I know you're busy and that you have competing interests for your time, but your story will not be told unless you sit down and write it. So schedule your writing time in the same way you reserve tee times at the golf course and play dates with the grandkids. Let writing have some presence in your schedule.

Next, designate a writing place. Whether it's done in a booth at the coffee shop or at a mahogany desk in your home office, your life story writing deserves a meaningful station in your environment. You're not just writing any story. You're writing *your* story, so write it someplace where you feel contented and productive and maybe even supported by a kind barista. Write where you feel—uplifted.

Fourth, get feedback. Find someone whose opinion you respect, and ask that person to comment on your writing. If you get good advice, take it. If this person tries to change your voice or rewrite your truth, then graciously run away as fast as you can. Remember. It's your story, and it's perfect.

Finally, remember that writing doesn't have to be a solitary practice. You don't have to do it alone. So find a writing group—or even a writing partner—if you need a community, and then welcome the opportunity to connect with people as quirky and as dedicated as you. Listen to each other's stories. Encourage each other. Help each other write.

And make sure someone brings the cookies.

ASSIGNMENT

What steps can you take to ensure that you will continue to write your life story? How are you scheduling your writing? Where does your best writing occur? How are you staying connected with other writers who can support your work and give you feedback? How does it make you feel when you're writing your life story?

CHAPTER 13

"How wonderful
it would be
to read stories
of my mother's life,
but it's too late for that.
Perhaps it's not too late
for me."

- Kay Teeter

Congratulations! You have begun writing your life story!

Along the way, I hope you've come to realize that life story writing isn't as difficult as you may have originally believed. In fact, maybe it's even enjoyable. So keep remembering, and keep writing. You will never regret reliving and recounting your life.

But would you mind doing something for me? Would you please tell your family and friends about your life story writing? Maybe they will be inspired to start their own stories if you tell them what we learned together here:

- Our lives amount to more than a collection of photographs. Make sure you leave behind something more substantial than a picture.
- Don't worry about your writing skills. Just write like you talk. After all, it's not the writing that really matters. It's your stories that we care about.
- In your story, you don't have to account for every minute of your life. Just write about a single event from your past. And then do it again. That's how this works—you write one story at a time.
- You don't have to be famous to have lived a life worth sharing. Some of the best memories are about the ordinary activities of daily living. And don't forget how much your stories will matter to your family—even generations from now.
- Your memories might be a little fuzzy, but it's surprising how quickly they come back when you start paying attention to your environment. We all have at least one memory that's stored in the smell of a campfire or the taste of a fresh-picked tomato.
- Once you've written a few stories, you may want to work with an expert to collect them into a book or other form. But if you write about only one or two memories, you will have accomplished much.

- Your writing matters. It makes you feel better when you do it, and your stories are a gift to those who read them. So set aside a time and place to write, and seek the company of other writers who will encourage you.
- Life story writing offers unexpected rewards. Not only does it allow you to enjoy your life again, it offers you another perspective on that life. In this reflection, magic can happen.

Section 2

LIFE STORIES

In the pages that follow are memories written by participants in my life story writing program.

Ranging in age from 48 to 85, these writers voluntarily submitted their stories for inclusion in Then · Again so that you could see how the techniques in this book can lead to real results.

Enjoy reading and reminiscing!

THE BEST THINGS IN LIFE

- by Kathy Carter

When asked what part of my life has been the best, my answer is, "I don't know." Not because my life hasn't been good. I just find it hard to identify what makes my life better or worse than anyone else's. So all I can do is describe some flashes of memory from my childhood.

I remember Dad whistling while he puttered around the house. The melodies would flow one after the other: Big Band tunes, college marches, and old standards like "You Are My Sunshine." Sometimes he would sing, but mostly he would whistle. I always felt happy when I heard those tunes, because it meant that he was happy too.

I remember walking with Mom from our home up Main Street when I was very small. We went into the Milk Depot, a small store that had a giant milk carton on top of the roof. I held Mom's hand on the way to the store and back again. She made me feel safe.

I remember eating meals with my family in the kitchen. With one leaf lowered, our table formed a half-circle against the wall. I sat in the middle, with my brothers and parents on both sides of me. I knew we would always have enough to eat, and we would always have each other.

I remember Mom working in the kitchen. She planned the menus and prepared the meals with care. I loved almost everything she served to us—except canned asparagus, which smelled terrible to me. But so many other foods she prepared were delicious: meat loaf with bacon on top, chicken and rice casserole, and pot roasts that made the whole house smell wonderful on Sundays. And her homemade cookies were my favorite.

I remember Mom teaching us kids how to follow recipes. She recruited my brother Gary to decorate the Christmas cookies, and she helped me make individual salads that looked like bunches of grapes. I knew that she wanted us to learn how to take care of ourselves.

I remember playing outside with neighborhood kids on summer evenings, watching for the street lights to come on. That was my signal to go home. If I didn't get home on time, Mom would stand at the front door and call my name. Then I knew I'd better get home quick.

I remember the empty lot next to our house. For my older brothers, it had been a makeshift baseball diamond for neighborhood games. For me, years later, it was my own country to explore. I would walk through the tall weeds, and in my imagination, I was an explorer stalking wildlife in the jungle.

I remember riding my bike, a blue Schwinn. After Dad took the training wheels off, I could ride up and down our street, and eventually around the block. I remember the feeling of freedom as I whizzed along with the breeze blowing my hair. One day I turned to look behind me, ran into the back of a parked car, and fell off. An adult that I didn't know came out of her house and made sure I was okay. Even away from home, I felt safe.

I remember one summer after my older brothers had left home for college. I put an electric typewriter on the desk in their room in front of a window, and that became my writing room. I could explore my ideas about journeys to faraway places, but I was safe at home.

I remember walking into the cornfield that grew behind our house. I felt like I was exploring a strange land. But when I wanted to come home again, all I had to do was turn around and follow the row back home.

All of these memories remind me of what was good about my childhood. I had the freedom to explore. And I had the stability of a home and family to come back to. Most important of all, I always knew that I was loved.

THE LAST MEAL

by D.L. Smith

I drove from Peoria to Pittsfield, Illinois, on a sunny Saturday morning in January of 1979 to visit my mother for the last time. Her cancer was relentless. Mom was in the acceptance phase; she had never wasted much time in the denial or anger stages. The three-hour trip was under a bright winter sun, all light and no heat.

Pittsfield, in western Illinois, was a typical small rural town, where a modest part of the town's population consisted of retired farm couples that found "moving to town" the prudent and necessary thing to do when their farming days were over. Mom was to be transported to the hospital today for care in her last days; the conventional practice of the 70's.

When I parked in the driveway I realized I had arrived ahead of my brother, Lawrence, and sister, Rose Anne. They had been there, but no doubt had errands to run. As I opened the front door, Mom somehow knew it was me. She greeted me in a faint voice from the bedroom, "Donnie, come in; I'm glad you're here."

Our words of greeting were soft and slow; few were needed. I removed my coat and entered the bedroom where she rested in the bed she had shared with Dad for 46 years.

She said proudly, "Donnie, I fixed you a meal so you won't have to stop to eat going home." I protested, "Mom, how did you do that? You're not supposed to be getting out of bed and moving around by yourself!" "I had a little energy this morning." she said with a smile, "Go out and see."

I walked back to the dining area that held our old farm family table. With the leaves removed it just fit into the corner between the kitchen and the front room. A sandwich containing lunchmeat and a slice of cheese, divided in two by an angled cut from corner to corner, rested on a kitchen plate. Two carrot sticks and a radish shared space on the plate, and an empty glass for a coke or water stood beside it. Mom's last meal was for me!

I stood and ran my hands along the side of the table and thought of all the grand meals that table had held. I remembered those abundant summer Sunday dinners when the table was heaped with fried chicken, mashed potatoes and gravy, fresh beans and tomatoes and carrots and beets, and all the other marvelous garden and orchard produce.

We always ate supper together as a family. With the symmetry of three boys and three girls, we sat in the same places every night, Mom at one end, Dad at the other. On one side sat John Edward next to Dad, then me in the middle, and Lawrence next to Mom. On the other side sat Margaret, Rose Anne in the middle, and Mary Jo next to Mom.

This old table was the altar of our family life together. Mom spread dress patterns on it, we did our homework around it, Dad worked his farm records on it. These pictures from the past floated through my memory, until my mom's call released me from them and brought me back to her bed. People would be coming soon. What could I say? What should I do?

Mom solved that. "Donnie, join me in the rosary I've been praying," she said. So I knelt beside her as she continued, "Holy Mary, mother of God, pray for us sinners now and at the hour of our death, amen."

The phrase "hour of our death" has relevance as never before. This prayer would be our private good-bye because we hear a knock at the door. Mom looks at me and then turns her head to look at the pillow beside her as we hear the sounds. I kiss her cheek and stand up. The next thing I know, Mom is gone. Rose Anne and Lawrence leave with her, accompanying the ambulance, and I'm alone.

I return to the bedroom and stand there. My gaze takes in the dresser, the chest of drawers, and the old black cast iron Singer sewing machine that sits just inside the door. At last I look at the bed where Mom had slept with Dad for 46 years—the bed where I had been conceived. I turn and softly close the door.

810 PERRY STREET – SANDUSKY, OHIO

- by Thomas S. Howard

Summer vacations with my grandparents were fertile ground for memories. When you travel out of the usual, it is an adventure, filled with new and familiar smells, sights and sounds that help form the foundation of a family, stories, and memories. Periodically, back in the routine, a smell, sight, or sound will appear and will take you back instantly to a place, time, and situation that only you can appreciate. I have only fond memories of my youth, of my summer vacations, and of our family adventures.

My maternal grandmother was Antoinette Gertrude Schnaitter. As a German, she was a very hardworking and thrifty lady. She also had a "green thumb," and she kept it very busy. My Uncle Frank had built a 4x8 foot greenhouse on the south side, so that "Nettie" could force the amaryllis bulbs early and lengthen the short northern Ohio growing season. Even in summer, when the glassed incubator was empty of plants, the aroma of potting mix and fertilizer blended with the summer sun and drifted like an earthy fog throughout the home.

The homestead was a combination of a couple of houses built with friends and family. Nettie and my Grandpa Smith had literally expanded the house as the family grew. All the hallways were narrow, floors sloped slightly, and rooms were irregular, as if their builder friends were only related to carpenters. The living room was quaint, with a low ceiling about 6' 6" and small for a family of 6. An ornate fireplace, at one end, seemed to emit a fond wet ash-like fragrance year round. As a child, I just remember feeling cozy and secure in that room. To me, the whole house was just filled with character. Christmas gifts were always placed on the oak bench in front of the fire, because there was no room for all the relatives and a Christmas tree!

The stairs to the basement were very steep, and I remember that, as a child, I was told to turn around and go down backward into the tiny native stone cellar. The primitive shower was also the handy work by my Uncle Frank, when he wanted privacy from his sisters. He used a Pears glycerin bar soap that he had special ordered from a confectionary out east. Half used bars where left precariously balanced on adjacent irregular foundation stones. Every so often during our stays, someone would open the basement door and allow the glycerin fragrance to escape as if it was lighter than air.

But it was Nettie's garden that was intoxicating. I have always been spellbound by the smell of boxwood on a warm summer night. Having been groomed for nearly 50 years, the scents of the various flowing plants would tag alone with you as you walked the path. It had been designed for strolling, with each path having annuals and perennial plants on either side and meandered out and back and around lazily. Nettie worked it constantly. She was on her knees most of the time and usually no gloves. The family photo album has a few posed family shots but pictures of Nettie usually included the garden. Those pictures speak volumes of a simpler place and time. I feel very fortunate to have shared time with a great family. Virtue and values develop in an individual from a variety of sources. Many are from example. Nettie probably never realized that what she was cultivating in the garden was far more than plants.

TOMAHAWK CREEK

- by Jack Brejc

I didn't spend much time alone with my Dad unless we were working on a home improvement project, and I was his helper. During those projects, the one-sided conversations were about which tool he needed next or how I should hold a trouble light so he could see better.

But, one day Dad and I went hiking. It was probably his idea since I never would have dreamed he would agree to go. We started by driving out Joliet Street north of LaSalle past Tobler Trucking where Uncle Johnny worked as a dispatcher. We honked. As we turned onto the first gravel road past St Vincent's Cemetery, I remembered riding my bike this way keeping far to the right in the gravel shoulder. I was more apprehensive this time about what would happen and what we would do since I didn't think Dad knew how to hike.

It was one of those dead-still Midwest summer days when dust billowed from our tires and floated in brown clouds that we drove back through after we turned around. The humid air was thick, so I was sweating just sitting in the front seat of our green Plymouth.

He parked in the driveway at the entrance gate to Mitchell's Grove. I never knew if that was the official name of this area or if we just started calling it that because the Mitchells lived directly across from the gate. They never bothered us or told us to leave through countless summer days of creek-wading, crawdad-catching, and tree climbing.

I showed Dad how to squeeze through the gap between the gate and the post like kids would do after hiding their bikes in the ditch. We crossed a waist-deep grassy meadow zig-zagging through the cow pies and hiked along the shore of the creek. I could smell that distinctive musty odor of the mossy, rancid mud as it stuck to our shoes and built up an inch-thick. We crossed a couple times at spots that were still and smooth and offered convenient stepping stone bridges.

But soon Dad wanted to get across at a deeper and faster running rapids. He took off his shoes and socks and rolled up his pant legs. His skin was very white from never wearing shorts. I was afraid of the current and rocks at this crossing, and he said he would carry me on his back. I was surprised when he didn't act disgusted about it. In fact he was really kind and seemed willing to do whatever it took to make it easy for me.

Dad knelt down, and I climbed up his back and reached around his neck. I never knew his beard was rough. He boosted me higher for balance and put one arm around my legs. He picked his way across the rocky creek bed, unaffected by the current. Finally, we reached the other side where he set me down then clambered up the steep bank. The crossing opened up to an unexplored meadow bordered by a steep wooded area, and we waded into the coarse grass.

We followed the grass along the creek and continued further north of route 80 than we kids usually went. He said he remembered that area of Tomahawk Creek from his youth when he would hike here. I was secretly impressed that he knew this area and grateful for a new name for the creek. I would amaze the other kids with that fact the next time we came out here. The whole afternoon was a gentle, adventurous, child-like side of my Dad that didn't fit, and I never saw again.

I was in my late 50's when Dad died at 97. We never said we loved each other. He never told me he was proud of me. The hardness of his motherless youth and depression-era life had left him with minimal capacity to show emotion. But, one day he took me on a hike and carried me across the creek.

BACON EDWARDS'
BIRTHDAY PARTY

- by Merrill Buesing

You might think we were cruel to have ever called anyone Bacon. We didn't. It was just descriptive 'cause he was a big boy. So was his brother Lard! What was unusual is that they were probably the only two fat people we knew in those lean years of the depression.

Bacon was in Arlis' second grade class, and I think he had a crush on her. That is why he invited her to his "birthday" party. Arlis knew Mom would be more apt to say OK if she made sure I was invited too. So Mom bought and wrapped a gift, and we took our baths (on a Saturday morning), put on our Sunday School clothes, and walked into Lynd.

Even at my pre-school age, I thought it was a strange party. There were only a couple other kids there. The Edwards were very poor and lived above Roloff's grocery store on Main Street. It was just one large sparsely furnished room with bare floors. We played games I had only played outdoors before. Games like hopscotch and tag. It was a lot of fun.

And then we had the cake and presents (present). It was a very bad chocolate cake—all doughy and gooey. We couldn't eat it so we played with it—we made little balls and threw them at each other. And then someone discovered you could throw those little balls at the ceiling, and they would stick. It was great fun! We laughed until the milk came out our noses, and then that became the new game. It was a wonderful party.

I don't know how we knew when it was time to leave, maybe when all the cake had been stuck to the ceiling. Arlis, in her extra maturity and wisdom, was having some second thoughts on the way home and suggested that we not tell Mom everything, but I was giddy and anxious to blurt it all out.

Mom wanted to know what presents Bacon got and I said, "Oh, we were the only ones that brought one. The other kids didn't know it was his birthday." She wanted to know how we got to be such a mess and didn't we know we had to wear those clothes to Sunday School the next day? So I told her how much fun we had with the cake. She was incredulous. "Where was Mrs. Edwards while all this was going on?" "Oh," I said, "she wasn't there. It was just a kids' party. Bacon even made the cake himself."

We got quite a lecture about our lack of judgment, our lack of maturity, our lack of manners, our lack of common sense, our lack of respect for other people's property, etc. etc. etc. I did not pay close attention to the part about what to do if we were ever in that situation again, because somehow I knew I would probably never attend another party quite like Bacon Edwards' Birthday Party.

THEN · AGAIN

OUR CHOICE

- by Mary Margaret
(Pete) Rich Maynard

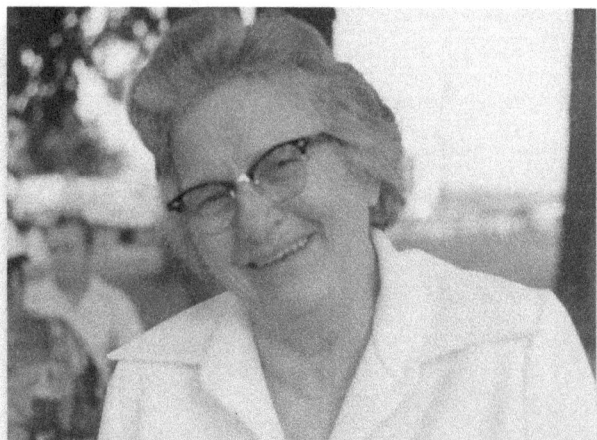

We thought we would
Landscape our yard -
And so we tried
So very hard
To form a plan
And a color scheme
Like we'd always pictured
In our dream.
So we pick up the rake
And the hoe
And out in the backyard
We go.
We'd plant some flowers
In front of the hedge
But that is the backdrop
For the stage
Where the girls dress up
And put on shows
And it costs a penny
For anyone who goes.
So we find another spot
That looks first rate
But we can't dig there
That's home plate!
So we move over
In another direction
Alas! that's the place
For the cheering section
For the football field
That occupies
Threefourths of the yard's
Total size.

79

And to dig over here
Would be such a shame
It's such a good place
For a marble game.
So we finally give up
Our flower bed
And decide to watch
Kids grow instead.

THEN · AGAIN

MR. WHEEL
AND THE CHEATER

- by Ken Maurer

I took the note from Mr. Wheel and headed out the door and down the hall to the Principal's office. The note said I want this kid out of my class and failed for the year. He is a liar, a trouble-maker, a cheater, and a smart aleck.

I tried to tell him to give me the tests orally. He did not even ask why. I got an "A" on the first test. He said next time I needed to show my work. I told him he would not be able to read it. I don't mean to, but sometimes I write backwards or upside down. He wanted it anyway.

"I treat every student the same. I teach them the same. I give every student the same amount of time to learn the material, and I certainly expect every student to take the test in the same way."

"But I can do it in my head. I don't need to write it down."

"Well, you do in my class. Do you have a degree in mathematics from a university?"

Before I could answer, he followed up with a couple of more questions.

"Have you ever taught algebra? Have you ever taught anything?"

"No...nope...and not really."

I got every answer right on the second test. He gave a me "C" cause he could not read my work. He called it gobbly-gook and said there was no possible way I could have got the answer correct unless I cheated.

On test number three, he had me move my desk to face the corner of the room.

"I will be watching you, and I want to see how you worked the problems."

I got them all right again. I liked algebra.

He threw the test on my desk and yelled.

"You cheated. I am tired of your foolishness."

"No. I did not...Mrs. Jones, my fifth grade-teacher, told me to ask you to give me the test orally."

"Am I a fifth-grade teacher? Am I Mrs. Jones? Do I look like Mrs. Jones?" he said with his arms crossed and glaring at me.

"No, no, and nope she is much fatter than you are."

I guess that is when he added smart aleck to my list of crimes.

I handed the note to the Principal's secretary. I saw her eyes get bigger when she read it.

"Oh my."

Mr. Patterson, the Principal, looked over the top of his glasses as he read the note.

"These are pretty serious charges. What do you have to say about them?"

"Well, I have told a fib or two. I might cause a little trouble sometimes, and I am not smart enough to be a smart aleck, but I am not a cheater."

He put his hand on his chin and narrowed his eyes,

"Then how do you explain getting all the answers correct?"

"I do them in my head the way my Dad does. I try to write down my work, but after I do it, the letters and numbers move. They don't move in my head."

"Let me see your algebra book." I handed it to him. "What chapter are you on?"

He opened the book and asked me three problems one at a time. I looked up in the air and worked them in my head. I got them all right. "See. I am not cheating. My Dad says I need to take algebra. Can I go back to class? I don't wanna disappoint my Dad."

A GREEN SHIRT

by Belevia Gibson

I pull the green shirt to my face embedding my nose deep within its folds. I breathe in its smell, a mixture of soap and something that is distinctly and totally him: a familiar smell I used to breathe each night as we lay sleeping.

The scent of soap thrusts me back in time. Art enters the bedroom looking fresh and energetic. His body is still hot and steamy from his shower. Little droplets of water cling to the fringes of his dark wet hair. The light source comes from the left and contrasting areas of shadow and light alternate on his face. He smiles at me with that shy, little boy smile that makes me want to go to him and ruffle his hair with my fingers. A white towel is draped around his middle. His skin is fair, almost delicate—neither sheer nor harsh, but composed of soft and light flesh tones. In his posture, I sense vulnerability and see tenderness in his eyes.

"I like being married," I think. "I especially like being married to him." Not only is he handsome, he is kind and loving.

I lay upon our bed on my stomach looking up at him and grin. "I think you're wonderful."

He comes and lies upon our bed on his stomach, his face close to mine. I smell the soap upon his skin and in his hair. The whiff creates an effect of freshness, of cleansing, of renewal. I surrender to the urge to touch him. I reach over and gently rumple his hair scattering the water droplets that hug his hair.

"Wait until you see the bathroom," he teases.

I lean into him, my forehead touching his. I gaze directly into his eyes. "I will still think you are a great man."

I remove the shirt from my face and sit down in the nearby chair. The shirt forms a mound of green in my lap. A sob begins to grow in my throat. I cover my mouth with my hand hoping to smother the sob, but it escapes. Tears form in my eyes. Loss fills me like smoke in a closed room.

Gingerly I lift the green cloth and rub it against my cheek. The fiber of the fabric feels as if someone's opened palm was upon my skin, and the top of my cheek feels cold and hot at the same time. I smell the fragrance of his essence. It is the scent I encountered when I would lean in and bury my head in his chest. The near closeness would release his scent and intensify his presence.

Sometimes I would seek his chest for comfort. When standing, my head would rest upon his breastbone. Like a pillar of bedrock, his chest provided me safety and security. Sheltered, as in a cliff of a rock, he covered me with his arms, and I would feel warmth and protection.

More often, I just wanted to breathe him in. When he would be sitting or lying down, I would come to him and nestle in his arms burrowing my head into his chest like a mouse in cotton linen. I inhaled his aroma. I would feel his heart beating. We talked about our lives, about work, our friends, about our two-year-old son. Then, slowly as minutes passed by, we would become silent. Not an uncomfortable silence but a silence that drew us in closer together. The silence was warm and gentle and alive. It was a safe silence without fear or suspicion or dread. Perhaps it was a holy silence for it enabled seeing beyond disposition or temperament and revealed the greatness and beauty of the person—which was the basis of our love.

I MISS HIS CHEST.

Gradually I lay the shirt down.

It is midnight, and I cannot sleep. I am alone in the big bed. The branches outside the window scrape against window pane. I stare at the ceiling for a long time recalling moments that were part of my married life. I close my eyes and try to conjure up the fringe of his hair, his smile, his laugh, the feel of his hand on the small of my back, his dark edged glasses always smudged. I am afraid I will forget him. What if I forget what he looks like?

I reach across to the empty side of the bed. Beside me lays the green shirt. I pick it up and bring it to my nose.

This is what I know. One day I was married. We were a family of three. Our faces were turned toward the future. There was a car accident. My husband was killed. There are now two of us.

TIME MACHINE

- by Barb A.

It was 2013 when I started the class, "Writing Your Life Stories," and I feel like I climbed into a time machine, going back in time, and living my life over but with acceptance and understanding.

I see that little girl, born on election day in 1932 in Grand Forks, North Dakota, on her mother's parents' farm in the middle of a blizzard during the great depression to a 29-year-old school teacher who hated teaching and an itinerant farm hand suffering with a disease called alcoholism.

My Mom later said, "Barbara is so impatient. Do you know she couldn't even wait to be born? She came early and had to be delivered by my aunt instead of the doctor."

I see the "agony and the ecstasy" of that little girl's life, her unhappy childhood, her good, kind, loving husband, raising six wild and wonderful kids, who are age 48 through 62 now. I see her jobs, starting as a babysitter at age 9, nanny at age 14, maid during high school, private secretary, stay-at-home mom, college student, registered nurse, world traveler, and happy content old lady at 82.

I see how the challenge of alcoholism touched our lives and our kids and how lucky we are to have survived to be a happy, cohesive, loving family, starting with our 8, and now our 22. I am still in this "Time Machine" and loving where it is taking me, through all 81 years.

A GOOD DAY

- by William Holt

My son, Jon, was with us for a short visit at our family cabin near Leadville, Colorado. He had been busy hiking with school friends, but they had returned home. Now he could spend his few days with his parents and grandmother.

Son, Ben, was flying in from Hawaii. His wife went to Tokyo to show off their new baby to her family. Ben would visit us for a week and then go to Tokyo. Jon and I were picking up Ben at the 2PM airport shuttle from Denver. I told my wife, Linda, that we should be back to the cabin by about 3PM. We waited only a short time, enjoying the view of the mountains, red dying beetle-killed pines, and the rear of the Safeway and Walmart®.

When Ben arrived, Jon suggested a quick trip up the pass towards Fairplay. He liked that area and wanted to take some pictures with his new camera. Ben is a good photographer and would take pictures too. I called Linda—we should be at the cabin about 4PM.

The lighting and clouds made for great photos. Jon is interested in clouds—he has the *Cloudspotters Guide* book and knows the names of ALL the formations. The boys were busy catching up; they hadn't seen each other for a year. Jon suggested that we continue on through the South Park area and return via Buena Vista. We took more photos of South Park ranchland and weathered buildings. I called Linda—we might be as late as 6PM.

On the way we took a scenic side road. Jon remembered that there was a grove of limber pines and bristle cone pines a few miles nearby. We found the path to the pines. It went across squared off logs over a stream, up through some aspens, up steeper switchbacks, and across a rock fall area. There were occasional little trail markers to show the way if we could find them. Dad was a little slow on the steep trail.

These pines are ANCIENT and REALLY interesting. They have gnarled, mostly bare trunks, with little wisps of green. Some look dead, but aren't, and make for great photos. Jon is doing graduate work in

93

biology, and Ben has always been interested in natural science, so there was much discussion about the conditions for trees to grow so slowly, but survive so long at this one particular place. I called Linda from the top of rock fall path—we will catch a meal on the way home and be at the cabin about 9 PM.

Just before Buena Vista, the highway winds through a small pass. There was a thunder storm. More clouds. The boys took lots of photos from the moving car. We stopped to look at sunset lighting over the prison water tower. Maybe we can catch a lightning bolt (we did). Oh look, several deer jumping a fence, but pretty far away. The photos revealed one doe and two 10-point bucks. Look at the light on those cliffs across the valley.

It was about 8PM when we looked for food in Buena Vista. Normally we eat lunch at the mom & pop café or the tea room, but this was dinner time, and Jon is vegan, so not just any place will do. (Ben had been a vegetarian, but one day he realized that he wasn't when he noticed that he was gnawing ham off a bone.) There is a nice restaurant in the old downtown area, but the folks on the sidewalk said that it was closed for a private event they had attended—they were carrying a few leftover unopened wine bottles. They said that the gas station was the best bet for a vegan.

An old gas station a few blocks away had been converted into a trendy gourmet place. We had an excellent meal, and had a good time discussing what we saw. It had been a good day doing something that I enjoyed with two of my sons that I don't see very often.

Before we pulled out I called Linda again—told her we had to eat at a gas station, but we'd be home in an hour. We arrived about midnight.

ODE TO P

- by Carol May

I've only known P for twenty-seven months. He's three feet tall, weighs thirty-eight pounds, has lots of curly brown hair and big brown eyes. So far we haven't talked about *The Great Gatsby* or the plight of the Syrian people or the meaning of life. Given the difference in age, it's unlikely we ever will. Right now we're having great fun watching *Thomas the Train* and *Bob the Builder* on *YouTube*.

For a good part of my life just having fun or savoring the moment or being totally goofy has been out of my reach. I can't recall a time when I didn't have a to-do list in front of me, or a schedule to create, or some sort of requirement to meet.

When I was thirteen years old, I was diagnosed with Type I diabetes. At the time I was released from the hospital, the internist who oversaw my care gave me a stern warning. He told me that young people with Type I diabetes didn't live very long unless they stayed on a schedule, and counted carbs, and monitored their glucose levels carefully, and took their injections faithfully. I took his admonition very seriously that day and have been on duty ever since.

That is, until P was born a couple of years ago ... something happened I can't explain.

After looking at thousands of pictures of my friends' grandchildren and hearing all of their "cute" grandma stories, I promised myself that if I ever had a grandchild, I would retain a sense of proportion in my life.

However, from the first time I held P, reason and sanity were cast aside. Now whenever he's around, schedules and to-dos are out. Zany and goofy are in.

We usually spend time on the floor playing with the remote control car that Poppa bought him for Christmas. The best part is when P pushes the button and drives the car into the baseboard, and we giggle at the "siddy" thing. Sorry, P can't say "silly" yet. That doesn't matter.

Or, we bring the keyboard down from its spot on the shelf and sing songs. His favorites are "*Twinkle, Twinkle, Little Star*" and "*Row,*

Row, Row Your Boat." I prefer "*The ltsy-Bitsy Spider.*" I can't sing, but P doesn't seem to care!

We also love to curl up on the sofa with the iPad and watch *Thomas* on *YouTube.* We've learned how to do train whistles, too. I don't think our noises sound like a real train, but so what!

But probably the most fun is when we throw on our coats, get in the car, crank up the heater, and drive off to the "aeroport" to watch the "pwanes" and "copters" take off and land. What can be more exciting!

After we get home, we share a bowl of ice cream. Some of it ends up on our faces or the floor. I'm not supposed to eat ice cream, but I just take an extra squirt of insulin and don't fret about it.

Here's to you, P. I'm in your debt for helping me be a kid again.

THEN · AGAIN

A WILKEN THANKSGIVING

- by Marilee Tilly

Entering the living room of Aunt Nita and Uncle Mart's house around noon on Thanksgiving Day in the 1960's, you first caught the smell of the cigarettes and perhaps the scent of the uncles' beer, a chattering football game backing their conversation, and the noise of cousins running through the rooms, accompanied by orders from the aunts: "Don't run in the house!"

Thanksgiving dinner was almost always at Aunt Nita's, as she had the biggest dining room and table. Going through the dining room to the kitchen, you noticed this table set with the good dishes and glasses on the shiny white tablecloth, and the children's card table in the corner.

In the small kitchen the aromas were tantalizing, the palette of food colors lovely. The best aroma was the huge baked turkey, cooling and waiting to be carved. Second best was the faint aroma of home-made bread and cinnamon rolls. Potatoes bubbled in the pot, almost ready to be mashed. Cranberries made from scratch were ready for the buffet in the dining room, along with one or more fruit salads, usually Waldorf and green Jell-O with pears. The green bean casserole and the cracker crumb-topped scalloped corn were ready, sharing oven space with the dressing. A relish tray with orange, green, red, and white hues of carrots, celery, radishes, and green onions would soon need refilling; this was the only munching allowed before the feast began. Out of temptation and harm's way in the bedroom were the pies: pumpkin, of course, at least two, accompanied by some combination of lemon meringue, apple, or mincemeat.

Each aunt had her task. Unmarried Aunt Janet, who didn't cook, was given table-setting, water-glass-filling tasks. Aunt Hilda, the general, brought her salad and/or pie and then proceeded to boss the cooks, who mostly ignored her. My mom was usually making the gravy while Aunt Nita mashed the potatoes. At this point, Uncle Mart or my dad, coming into the kitchen for another beer, was pressed into carving the turkey. Aunt Ruth, with no children of her own, usually was putting filled dishes on the buffet and trying to supervise the younger cousins running through the house. As the only teenage girl, I tried to maintain a low profile, both to avoid being put to work and to listen to the gossip and memories the sisters loved to share.

The meal itself, after a quick prayer of thanks, was beyond description. Food aromas swirled, dishes clanked as they were passed around the table and then to the kids' table, and, except for that one brief moment of silence when everyone's plates were finally filled, and first bite taken, conversation and laughter and pure joy abounded. The aunts got up and passed refills, cleaned up kids' messes, and eventually everyone was groaning with full stomachs. Then came pie and coffee; most of the too-impatient younger kids were already outside playing.

The uncles and grandpa, full to the brim, returned to the living room to watch football, an excuse for a quick snooze. The ladies stayed at the table to talk for another half hour before facing the massive cleanup and dishes. Staying out of sight until dishwashing was well underway would get me the relatively easy task of carrying dried dishes back to the table. Somewhere around 6 pm, turkey, bread, condiments, and leftovers were put out for sandwiches, a prelude to the second piece of pie.

Those childhood Thanksgivings set the standard for me. Thanksgiving wasn't only the wonderful food; it was the love and bonds created by the aunts and uncles. It was about sharing memories made during the rest of the year: Christmas parties, picnics, fishing vacations together—memories that were a big part of the Thanksgiving conversation. My Thanksgivings today are very different, of course, but I wouldn't trade a minute of the Thanksgiving meals I grew up with.

THEN · AGAIN

THE BOX

- by Mary L. (Mariel) Spahr

As they say . . . simple pleasures. Well, that sums up what the box meant to me. It was an ordinary paper box, but nicer than a brown cardboard box. The kind you used to get at a fine department store when you purchased something like a hat or lingerie. It was sturdy not flimsy, and white with a shiny finish. The lid lifted off from the top and when replaced slid all the way to the bottom. It was square, maybe twelve by twelve and about half that high.

As a child I was thrilled when the box was brought out. It didn't happen regularly, and that's the way it should be. If you can have something all the time it isn't as special. Mom used to refer to the cliché: Absence makes the heart grow fonder. That's what the box was like for me.

It was stored high on a shelf in our spare room closet. Funny, as much as I enjoyed it, it never crossed my mind to take it down without permission. Mom was always the bearer of the box.

What was inside? Well, it truly was simple . . . it was full of scraps. I loved digging through it, which stirred up all kinds of creative ideas that would start spinning wildly through my head! Bits of rickrack, pieces of lace, yarns, sequins, colored cotton balls, tiny scraps of fabrics (velvet was a real prize), random buttons, feathers, pipe cleaners, little plastic roly-poly eyeballs, glass rhinestones, and other such wonderful things! Oh, and I can't forget the little jars of glitter. They were made of glass back then and had metal lids with pierced holes. A piece of cardboard guarded the holes until you were ready to shake the glitter out like salt. My favorite was when Mom would combine leftovers into one jar of multi-colored glitter.

Nothing was ever thrown away in a home headed by children of the depression. Mom and Dad always said you should save things because you never knew when you might need them, or they would come in handy. It was always fun to speculate what assortment of miscellany may have been added since the box was last out, so there was anticipation and mystery associated with the box, too.

When was the box brought out? Sometimes it was merely a special treat on a rainy day, a welcome opportunity to randomly create. Other times it was expected, like when coloring Easter eggs. After the eggs were dyed, out came the box. I would sit at the kitchen table for hours decorating egg after egg, each one completely different with its own unique design. I remember being proud of them all, and I couldn't wait to place them on the table Easter Sunday!

The box, such a simple thing, yet it holds a very special place in my childhood memories. Many hours of enjoyment were had from that box. I'd like to think it is a timeless kind of pleasure. Maybe, just maybe, one of my grandchildren will find my own box of scraps worthy of their curiosity, time and creativity, amidst a world of high tech toys and games.

A STEEL MAGNOLIA

- by Laurie Hartshorn

"I don't feel good, Mommy," said my preschooler.

She had been fighting tonsillitis and running a low-grade fever, but seemed to be getting better. As I changed her into fresh pajamas and got ready to tuck her into bed, I noticed something that caused a bubble of fear to rise in my chest. There on her little neck was a lump the size of a jawbreaker. Both my mind and stomach were churning with dread as I settled her in bed surrounded, maybe even protected, by the comfort of her books and stuffed animals while I conjured up all the horrible childhood illnesses that lump could signal.

My call to the pediatrician secured a prompt appointment, but there was still time for panicked worrying seasoned with plenty of maternal blame. How had I missed such an obvious sign of illness? Only a truly rotten mother could have been so oblivious to her child's condition. How would I cope if my worst fears were realized?

Then I remembered how my own mother had dealt with a similar situation. I must have been about six years old the summer that we spent in California. My father, a high school teacher, was working on his doctorate and was taking courses at UC Berkeley. An added bonus for my mother was that her two sisters lived nearby, and she would have the pleasure of their company all summer long. My sister and I would have six little girl cousins to play with as well.

We drove cross-country from St. Louis, a journey I remember very little of, and rented basic campus housing hurriedly slapped up for returning veterans making use of the G.I. Bill. I remember happy times of wading in the Pacific and playing with my cousins. But mid-summer I became deathly ill.

My worried mother consulted with her sisters who recommended their trusted pediatrician. When she called for an appointment, she was told that the doctor was not taking any new patients. My mother was a genteel southern lady who was unfailingly polite and soft-spoken. Being gracious and mannerly were her default settings. Aggressively browbeating the office staff until they surrendered would never have occurred to her.

But this was the summer of the polio scare, and she would have sacrificed herself rather than allow something to happen to one of her children. If this was the doctor her sisters thought was the best, then this was the doctor I must have. She wrapped me up, somehow got me to the doctor's office, and sat unyielding in the waiting room until they agreed to see me.

I was diagnosed, not with polio, but with a severe strep infection requiring strong antibiotics to be administered around the clock. My mother set her alarm and woke me for each dose. Because I was too little to swallow a capsule, she opened each one and coaxed me to swallow the bitter medicine by offering a sip of grape soda (a rare and special treat) after each dose.

I thought about my mother's example as I drove to the doctor's office with my own ailing daughter. When our familiar and trusted pediatrician examined her, his eyes met mine over her little blonde head. Then he uttered some of the sweetest words I have ever heard.

"This is not what you think."

She, too, had a strep infection that could be treated by the proper antibiotics. Relief swept over me in the same way it must have comforted my mother years earlier.

I remember very little of my long-ago illness and recovery. When I questioned my mother about it, she made it sound fairly commonplace and not a bit heroic. But I know the fear and helplessness she must have felt in the face of my illness, because I too felt it whenever my own child was sick.

How blessed I am to have had a southern belle with a spine of steel to mother me and to serve as my guide as I traversed the foreign country of parenthood.

A FEAST
FOR THE SENSES

- by Linda B. Holt

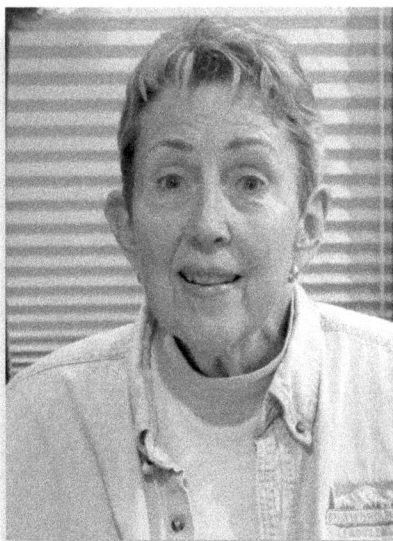

I step out onto the deck from the kitchen door. The afternoon is quiet after the thunderstorm and rainfall which moved across the valley. The soft smell of the pine trees is heavy with the damp air. The dust has been washed off the pine needles and bark of each lodgepole in the area, and the soil is a dark brown—so different from the usual dusty color that is the norm. My steps on the damp soft needle bed are nearly silent, and that fact adds to the overall quiet of the post-storm silence.

The breeze begins playing with the trees across the road and moves around the club slowly but steadily, leaving silence behind it and motion within it. It is cool and refreshing as it finds my face and hair. I walk down the road to the stream where the wind makes ripples on the open water and then moves on leaving quiet in its wake. It is so good to feel the dampness in an otherwise very dry air.

As I continue my walk I pass the ducks in the cove near the road, then the place where the beavers climb up the lake bank, cross the road, and then slide down into the meadow. The clouds above me begin to part and the Colorado blue sky starts to peek out, and then the sun grows warm and comforting on my shoulders. I am now on the old road by the cabins and have to watch my step lest I turn an ankle on a stone. I look out over the lake to the East and can again see the ridge across the valley. I see the breeze at work over on that ridge, and I hear birds getting busy and see chipmunks out again too. So the storm is really over and life gets back to normal in Home Stake Trout Club.

THE MAN IN THE RED SUIT

- by John J. McNally

It sounded like a good idea at first and then reality set in.

The original plan was for some enterprising pilot to participate in a Christmas celebration sponsored by the Chamber of Commerce in the small western Iowa town of Sloan. December of 1948 had arrived with cold temperatures and an unusual amount of snow. The plan went forward to drop Santa Clause from a light plane by parachute, have him land at the edge of town where the town fire truck would be waiting, and for Santa to then ride triumphantly into the town square distributing candy and other goodies to the waiting children along Main Street.

I was to learn later that several other pilots had declined to get involved in this scheme; however, for lack of common sense, I agreed to participate for the grand sum of $50. It seemed a fair compensation for about an hour's work. Besides, it sounded like it might be fun.

Santa wasn't really going to jump; we would stage it so he only looked like he did. It wasn't really Santa; it was to be a parachute test dummy dressed in a red suit. From a distance and a height of about a thousand feet, it would probably fool most of the people and all of the kids—or so we hoped.

On the appointed day, the weather failed to cooperate. It was snowing heavily, and the ceiling was below 1,500 feet. In addition, I had been planning to use my open cockpit biplane, a war surplus Stearman Trainer for the event. This was not the time to be cruising around in an open airplane, so I looked for an alternative. Most of my buddies wanted nothing to do with this mad scheme, but one of them, a seasoned pilot who had flown artillery spotters in the European Theater and could put a small plane through places that most people couldn't drive a car, agreed. Tommy would use his ski-equipped Piper Cub and split the fee with me.

A parachute dummy weighs 170 pounds and consists of a heavy canvas body with short arms and legs and a nub of a head, all bound in leather. From a distance, it could pass for a man so we strapped a backpack chute on him and crammed the three of us into the confined space of the Cub. We arranged ourselves so that Tommy sat in front in order to fly the airplane. I sat in the rear seat, holding the dummy on my lap with its stubby legs resting on each of Tommy's shoulders. Since it was so crowded with the three dummies in the cabin, we were unable to close the side opening enclosure and flew with it open.

We staggered into the air with this insane arrangement, managed to find the town of Sloan, made a couple of passes over the crowd, checked the wind direction and speed as best we could, and lined up to make the drop. At an altitude of about a thousand feet, we estimated a point that would put Santa on the ground close to where the fire truck waited.

We had tied a length of light rope to the step of the airplane and the other end to the parachute ripcord handle to provide a means of opening the chute once it left the door. In the process of struggling with the awkward arrangement out of the side of the Cub, the rope had become entangled and pulled the ripcord causing the chute to open prematurely. This left me with only one alternative—shove the whole package out of the door as fast as I could and hope that nothing got caught on the tail of the Cub. The fact that I survived to tell this story is sufficient evidence to prove that is what happened.

We watched to see the man in the red suit land fairly close to the target; now to get home. The weather had really closed down, so we decided to land in a farmer's field. We tied the airplane down and hitched a ride back to the airport.

On Christmas Day, Tommy and I spent an hour or more hand cranking the Cub which finally coughed into life just as the sun was going down over the Missouri River. We flew home chastened by our experience and grateful to have survived.

UP DAY

- by Vick Steward

In the genesis years of my manhood, it became apparent to me the effort my father made to learn about the substance of my life, more so than I did his. I was on pabulum-break when God handed out genes that entice a man to hunt, fish, to work on car motors. Those interests and talents by-passed me. Without grudge, my father embraced his male heir who shared few of his own sportsman's pursuits.

Mid-November 1967 found Dad terminally ill. Much of his time was spent in bed. I'd graduated from college a few months earlier and began a new job. Life was spinning ahead for me. It was winding down for Dad. We both had accepted that.

During his illness, Dad referred to a day on which he felt better as an "up day." He didn't have a name for those on which he felt punk. One afternoon, he announced it was an "up day" and said, "Take me for a drive. Bring your camera. We might see something."

When we reached the highway, I asked which direction he wanted to go. He pointed left and said, "Let's go check on that tree of yours."

Since there were many, I had to ask, "Which tree?"

"The one by the Brehm place" he specified. "The one you've shown me pictures of."

About fifteen miles from our home, near the highway, on a hill, stood the remnants of a massive walnut tree that had died five or six years earlier. The marriage of time and elements had stripped the tree of its bark and small branches. All that remained was a bleached bone carcass. Finding a simplistic beauty in dead trees, over the past decade I had photographed this one and many others in various seasons, light varieties, and angles.

The day was damp, grey-skied; a numbing nip of wind blew off a Midwestern iceberg. Late autumn rains filled the creek that tumbled between the highway and Dead Tree Hill. This small flood blocked my usual highway-to-hill hiking path. Surmising Dad's health condition didn't allow us to stop, this temporary obstruction of nature provided

119

an excuse not to pause.

He pointed to suitable parking along the highway's edge. "Why don't you stop?"

"Can't get across the stream."

"Course you can. Hike back a couple hundred yards and use the farm road entrance."

Dad remained in the car as I walked in the cold wind which seemed to sap what little of my already near-absent photography inspiration that existed that day. The camera and I filled a near half-hour snapping away, more to appease him than add to my cursory nature photos.

Finally, I waved to indicate that I was finished. Through the car window, Dad acknowledged my wave by lifting his hand barely above his shoulders. The gesture seemed to say, "I'm tired. Let's go home."

As I climbed into the driver's seat, for the first time I head-on comprehended the savagery being played out on my father's body by the disease that would eventually claim his life. His perfect fit hunting jacket now bulged with extra room across the chest. The cap, once nattily worn, slumped low over the top of his ears. Weight loss caused his hands to appear haggard, the once nimble fingers to look lame.

Commentary about past hunting episodes down fence rows we passed and fishing luck along creeks we crossed dominated his conversation during our drive home.

As we left the car in the garage, I said, "Was this rough for you?"

His thoughtful, tender response was, "No, it's fine. Seeing you enjoy yourself was good for me." That was to be our final outing.

I still have one of the photographs I snapped that day. From time to time, I retrieve it from a drawer and put it on my desk for a few hours, maybe a few days, sometimes for a week or two.

THEN · AGAIN

AFTER SCHOOL

- by Robert H. Yonker

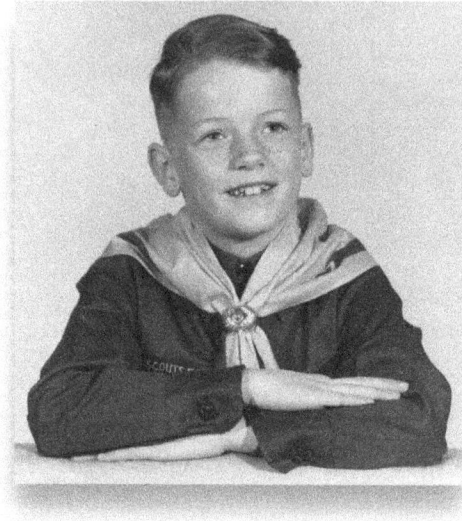

We played games until dark or until mother called us for dinner —which we always responded with "Mom, just five more minutes," — usually several times.

My favorite game was Eenie Einie Over with my best 5th grade friend, Dale. We played at his house, which was four doors down, because his house was lower (in height). We started playing the game with a tennis ball over his garage then graduated to throwing over his house. You throw the ball over the house shouting Eenie Einie Over when you throw. If the ball fails to go over you yell, "Pigtails" and try again.

If the ball does go over, Dale would try to catch it before it hit the ground. If he did catch the ball, then he would choose which way to run around the house and try to hit me with the ball. I would look for him and run the opposite way around the house to be "safe." Then it would be Dale's turn to throw.

One trick was to throw the ball, so that it would hit the roof over the doorway, thus causing it to bounce sideways and be harder to catch. We played to ten points to win a game. It was really hard to get points, because Dale was a fast runner.

One evening after playing Eenie Einie Over, Dale and I had our first camping adventure. We slept in a tent overnight... in his back yard. The tent was a small pup tent that barely contained our two sleeping bags. It was great. We could stay up and talk as long as we liked.

Later, we were dozing off when we heard a noise. It sounded like a deep raspy sound... and it was coming closer to our tent. There was also a rustling in the grass noise. "Snake!" Dale yelled pulling the sleeping bag over his head. I did the same.

Then it happened. Two snakes slithered into our tent onto our sleeping bags and grabbed us! It was my Dad who had snuck up on our tent, made the noises, and then reached in to grab us. He thought he was making frog noises so was very surprised at our screams and kicking. We all laughed so hard we cried... then tired, we quickly fell asleep knowing Dad would not let any snakes get us.

I don't remember camping again, but we played a lot more of Eenie Einie Over until Dale became very sick... he lost all his hair... and then Dale passed away.

Reflection: Enjoy those you love everyday as if it is you're last time with them. Sometimes it will be.

THEN · AGAIN

THE DEATH
OF A PRESIDENT

- by Sue N.

An irritating static sputtered from the intercom mounted above the door, disturbing the quietness of study hall on Friday afternoon, November 22, 1963. Mr. Morris, Mc-High's Principal, made an announcement:

"President Kennedy was shot while riding in a motorcade in Dallas today."

He didn't provide any details. Just a minor injury, I assumed. You could have heard a pin drop as, one-by-one, everyone bent their heads back down to resume their studies.

A half-hour later, as we were in the halls heading to our last class of the day, Mr. Morris' voice again boomed over the intercom. This time he was very specific:

"President John Fitzgerald Kennedy died at 1:00 p.m. CST today."

Everyone looked straight ahead, in absolute silence as we shuffled to our classroom. I had American History with Mrs. Dorothea B. Mrs. B. had the rare talent of making history come alive for high school students. Just a few days earlier, she had marched up and down the rows, waving a small flag, as she told us about her British-American dual-citizenship and her immigration from Jamaica to America. But on this afternoon, we talked about history so new that it hadn't even been written yet.

Cable television and 24/7 news broadcasts did not exist. Revered news anchors Walter Cronkite, Chet Huntley, and David Brinkley provided a half hour of news at supper time and again at 10:00 p.m. But the murder of a president was no ordinary circumstance. The network television stations immediately cancelled regular programming to cover the event.

That evening my family tried to absorb the events of the day as we watched television until it went off the air at midnight. We saw reruns of the Presidential motorcade making its way past the Texas School Book Depository in Dallas that morning, the jerking movements as the President and our Governor, John Connally, were shot, Secret Servicemen scrambling to assist. We saw Vice-President Lyndon Johnson sworn in as the thirty-sixth President of the United States aboard *Air Force One*, with the newly widowed First Lady Jackie Kennedy, still in her stained pink suit, standing glassy-eyed by his side. We saw Lee Harvey Oswald in handcuffs as he was arrested in a theater later that afternoon and charged with murdering the president.

News coverage continued throughout the weekend. We went to church on Sunday, but otherwise hunkered around our television watching events unfold. Conspiracy theories ran rampant, gaining more steam on Sunday evening, when Oswald was shot and killed on live television by a nightclub owner named Jack Ruby. Could the assassination be pulled off by one unknown, insignificant, person? Had someone hired Oswald to do the deed? Was more than one gunman involved? Did Ruby kill Oswald because of his profound grief over losing a beloved president, or did he kill Oswald to keep him from talking about some larger malicious plot?

As I was lying in bed Sunday night, I heard an airplane overhead. My imagination went wild.

We were in the middle of the Cold War. That could be a Russian plane. No doubt they wanted to take over our country. With our president lying dead, we were vulnerable. Was Russia involved in the assassination? Oswald had embraced Communism and had lived in Russia for a while.

For the first time in my life, I was afraid for our country.

President Johnson declared Monday, November 25, to be a national day of mourning. School was cancelled. Once again, we gathered around the television to watch President Kennedy's funeral. I was mesmerized by the beautiful but poignant ceremony: both dignitaries and common man lined up to view the casket in the Capitol Rotunda, the casket being carried by caisson to St. Matthew's Church, the riderless horse in the procession, three-year-old John-John saluting his father's casket as it was carried from the church.

On Tuesday morning the television networks resumed their regular programming, and I went back to school, forever changed.

SEPTEMBER 24, 2008

by Florence C. Beltz

I have given myself permission to have this afternoon, alone, to say good-bye to Jubilee Park. The Governor is closing it, on or about October 15. It is a very sad event. I can not grasp the logic of, or the fact that, this will no longer be available to me or anyone.

I came about 12:30 and parked on the circle as usual. No humans around. Only the bee buzzes and the screechy bluejays interrupting the summer quiet amidst the vibrant purple iron weed and glorious yellow goldenrod patches.

It is hot, and I walked slowly down the path to "my" pond. I couldn't find my hat in the trunk, and I needed it. Cell phone in pocket and good ole walking stick in hand, I just soaked up the quiet late summer activity by the side of the water. I saw frogs and fish jumping, dragonflies flashing turquoise shimmers, and one low flying duck. Even the 8-inch fish swam leisurely along, no hurry. No blue heron around either on this day.

When I got back to the car, I got some ice water and this writing pad and then attempted to cross the fence to a picnic table in the shade. Instead I fell, the ice water spilled, and all of my writing from yesterday was obliterated. That writing had been all about my attempts to forgive one of my brothers-in-law. When that effort was washed clean today, I truly felt God was telling me, "That's done, go forward from here."

So, I got back in the car, drove through the park, and I am now "on top," near the old church. I am also in the shade, in closer view of my car and many, many big wonderful trees. Good grief. I forgot my camera. There is a marvelous, spreading oak limb just to my right that could tell such stories. In my line of vision is the shelter where they had the marvelous stew and crafts at the autumn harvest festival. On my left a big maple is beginning its yellow gold.

Joyce would know for sure, but I think just down the hill is where I came to my first volleyball picnic with the club some 40 years ago. In the valley there The Ole English Faire was held. I enjoyed all the pomp and trumpets and jousting about. People were jolly when they came to that. Pat came with me there one year, and I found my big brimmed straw hat, after I was already sunburned. One year John and I sat on hay bales listening to the dulcimers.

Pat was also with me that snowy February afternoon that we got really lost walking the ski trail. I had visions of being there all night, then I glanced up and saw utility wires in the distance. It was dark when we got onto the hard road, miles from the car. Is that the last time she has come?

Gosh, the memories: the flock of Eastern bluebirds when Hilli was here, the fried chicken birthday picnic with my sister, the orange gold Baltimore oriole flashing in the sun and singing his happy trill, the very first sign of green in spring, finding the bluebird's nest in the campground, and the peace of that late evening October walk. I am so glad that I have been here for it all. And that this place was here for me.

I have been up here a zillion or so times by myself too in these Peoria years. Sometimes I just go back by the pond that is so like the area by the creek at home. I just soak up the beauty of the trees, grass, sky, and I marvel at those and God's wondrous creatures. Sometimes I just sit and stare. It is so peaceful here.

Oh, and there are blackberries, just at the entrance to the path to the pond! Henceforth, I guess the birds will get them all.

My pen and paper have often been with me. It is an excellent place for thinking—or not. I wrote some of my grief here when Robert died. I've done some journaling and made lists too. And worry sheets made and deposited in the handy barrels when I finish. That too is refreshing, to dump your worries.

It has started to thunder now. I'd best get out from under this tree.

I am so thankful for you Jubilee Park! I treasure the memories here and the realness of things alive in this natural wonder. I wish this peaceful place would last. It has soothed my soul to be here. Always.

LUNCH TIME
AT LIBERTY NO. 1

- by Flo Banwart

I knew something important was about to happen! My feet and hands had been scrubbed clean, and it was only Monday morning. It was a warm September day in 1950. This was the beginning of my formal education and it was to take place at Liberty No. 1, the small red brick schoolhouse just one-half mile from the farm where I grew up. It was the same one-room school my father and my Aunt Dorothy attended when they were in primary school. Going to school for the first time is a memory that everyone carries for a lifetime, and my first day of school is just such a memory.

The rural schools of Iowa were spread throughout the farms and were organized so no student had more than a two mile walk to the nearest school. Hancock County had schools that served all of the rural townships, including where we lived in Liberty Township. This was to be my school for the next seven years.

Along with everything else that was new for me that day, lunch time was a part of that grand new beginning. I was the eldest of three at that time, so I didn't have older siblings to tell me what was going to happen. I soon found out that lunch time was a noisy, smelly meal that broke up the school day.

When our teacher excused us for our noon break, everyone collected their dinner pails from the cloak rooms. The boys' room was on the right of the front hallway and the girls' room on the left. The lined up dinner pails were an assortment of metal containers that had been brought from home by each kid, some more carefully carried than others.

This dinner pail was an important part of our needed equipment when we got ready to go back to school in the fall. Dents and scratches marked each one and made it a personal part of our school supplies. The walk to and from home usually involved swinging it, twirling it, scraping it along the gravel when it was set down to investigate something interesting in the ditch, or throwing it on the bench in the cloak room or on the kitchen table.

My dinner pail was a large black type. You've seen them before, carried by men as they go off to work! When it was opened there was a big red Thermos® bottle in the top and room for lunch in the bottom. You can imagine the damage I waged on it through primary school. There were several Thermos® bottles, each replaced when broken, but that black dinner pail was the same one I carried every day for seven years. Many things became hand-me-downs, but this one thing stayed with me throughout my primary school days.

When it came time for that first meal at noon, I carried my dinner pail back to my desk at the front of the classroom. My classmate, Jimmy B., and I were the only kindergartners that year. All of the students were arranged with the youngest at the front and the oldest eighth graders, the big kids, at the back of the room. That year there were about 20 kids enrolled in the school.

I opened my dinner pail and had a look at what was there. My grandmother had packed my lunch, because my folks were on vacation in Canada. So, she saw to it that I had lots of good things to eat. There were homemade date cookies, a sandwich, a Thermos® of milk, and a banana. The item that I especially remember was she had carefully wrapped three olives in waxed paper. My Grandma knew what I really liked! To a 4-year-old kindergartener, that was the best part of my lunch. No doubt I ate them first!

Everyone had a pail filled with food, so as the afternoon began the room was filled with the smells of orange peels, banana peels, apple cores, and left over sandwiches filled with bologna or liverwurst. It must have been a "delight" to smell! Still today, whenever I smell a freshly peeled orange, I think of my days at country school! Miss H., our teacher that first year, must have had a strong stomach!

I remember very little about the details of that day, but the dinner pail that accompanied me to Liberty No. 1 School every day after that was a constant reminder that someone cared enough to pack something special to eat.

ENJOYING MY LIFE

- by Phyllis Marie Calliss

I am certainly enjoying this stage of my life for many reasons. One of the things I like best is the freedom. The freedom to come and go as I please, eat when I want, say yes or no to whatever.

My husband and I raised three children; we've been through the dance, music lessons, camps, proms, class trips, and three colleges. So, I feel we did our job as parents, put in our time so to speak.

It's as if there's a newfound freedom at this point. We like to travel, especially our yearly jaunt to Gulf Shores Alabama. That's one of the places snowbirds like to go to, of course Bill and I are only snowchicks. We stay in a condo right on the ocean with five other couples that are friends of ours from Washington. Needless to say, we have a wonderful time doing nothing important.

Sometimes I think it can be the really simple things in life that are so relaxing: a long walk on the beach, counting the stars, and listening to the never ending waves of the ocean. It has taken reaching this time of my life to be able to stop and enjoy life's simple pleasures. When we're young, working raising a family, life gets very complicated.

I also have the time in my life to enjoy gardening, working in God's glorious earth. It's almost a spiritual feeling to have my hands digging in the soil, smelling the dirt, and seeing the little creatures that flowers grow. I love to watch the transformation as they mature and grow. I have some of my best conversations with God when I'm digging in the dirt. I think he can really hear me without walls around.

Now for the very best reason for this time of my life, the Grandchildren. What a gift! It's hard to explain, but they are the absolute best ever. I love them all (6) to death, but I don't want to babysit them on a regular basis, because I want to be the fun Nana. You can't do that and raise them. I love when my own children tell me I let the grandchildren do things they didn't get to do. I laugh a lot.

This is the time to do the things I didn't have time for in my earlier years. This summer I learned to swim, 67 yrs old, so I decided to conquer that fear, feeling pretty proud. It was a big one on the bucket list. The next thing on the list is playing guitar, so I will start lessons soon.

These things aren't a big deal to some people, but they are to me and it makes me feel so good. Taking this class was also something I had wanted to do for a long time, just had to muster the courage. I'm so glad I did, it's given me the push to continue writing the stories of my life.

EXTRA! EXTRA!
HEAR ALL ABOUT IT!

- by Jeanne Buysee

What were my parents thinking, to let their nine-year-old daughter have a paper route? I applaud them for letting me take on my first job. The year was 1950, and paper girls were not the norm. Without knowing it, I was in the early stages of becoming what is now considered a women's libber, and a Tom Boy to boot. I resisted dolls, dresses, and all things feminine. I also had a penchant for wearing ball caps and a reputation for roughing up my male playmates when we re-created war events. A paper route was another avenue into the boy's world in which girls were looked upon in dismay, and not readily welcomed—a perfect place for me.

Having a paper route in those days was comparable to owning a small business. I delivered a product, collected the payment for it, and after paying the publisher, the remainder was my profit. Collecting for the paper was the most frustrating part of the job. Each customer had a card with each week of the year listed and when they paid, I would punch the proper date. Often I was not able to collect due to a customer not being home or not having the cash to pay me. If I did not collect enough to pay my weekly bill from the *Journal*, it meant that I did not receive all of my earnings that week. It also meant that I had to continually stop and try to collect from those slackers.

I loved the Christmas season, especially when it snowed, and I would have to walk and carry my papers. Paper bag slung over my shoulder, walking through the snow, and singing Christmas carols, as if I was Rosemary Clooney, are some of the best memories of my life. The paper bag had another purpose, to carry home the generous Christmas gifts from customers. The Lifesaver® book was as popular then as it is today, and I loved every one I received.

Like all proper businesses, the delivery people have a manager. Our manager's name was Mr. Jones, and he would occasionally show up at the pickup location to check up on the carriers. I was the only female paper carrier, which had never been an issue. But one day, as all of us

143

were at the paper drop off location, the boys were discussing a wonderful event that they had just experienced. I asked them about it, and they told me Mr. Jones had taken them all to tour the *Journal* plant and then to the Steak 'n Shake for lunch.

Missing a boring tour didn't bother me as much as the pain of not being included, especially for lunch at Steak 'n Shake! I then experienced my first "calling out" concerning something I considered unfair. The next time Mr.J. was in town to check on me, I asked him why I was left out of the trip. His curt and unforgivable reply, was, "Girls wouldn't be interested in that." I am not sure exactly what I replied, but the fact that it still stings has kept me mindful of the importance of equality.

My time as a paper girl was the one of the best experiences of my life. It gave me an understanding of human nature and the importance of working not only for money but for serving others.

THEN · AGAIN

SUNDAY DINNERS

- by Julie Paris

Sunday dinners always took place in the large dining room. The table was large enough to accommodate my four siblings and myself with Mom and Dad at each head. My two brothers sat across from my two sisters and myself. We all sat in order of age with me, the youngest, on my mother's left and my oldest brother on my father's left. There was a large veined mirror on the wall behind my brothers, and I could see myself when I was tall enough to do so when seated. Until then, I sat on a volume of the *Yellow Pages*.

Several sideboards lined the walls around the room. A small china cabinet held ruby red glass, silver salt and pepper shakers, a gravy boat that had belonged to Grandma Getzoff, and assorted decorative china. The large buffet behind my brothers held linens and silver. It had a silver service on it trayed in by brass rails around three sides. The server behind my mother was smaller with inlaid mahogany. It had drawers that held all kinds of wrapping paper and ribbons and cards, convenient when we used the table to wrap Christmas gifts. Behind us three girls was the bar buffet with all sorts of crystal decanters filled with liquors, their names announced on silver labels chained around the neck, and delicate etched martini and low and high ball glasses. Importantly, a carving table on wheels sat next to my father's chair. This is from where he served dinner.

Major preparations always took place in the afternoon before the early evening dinner. My mother sent my sisters and I out to the garden to pick the centerpiece for the table. Janice, my oldest sister, and I were in charge of setting the table. This was the one day a week that the sterling and best china were used. We artfully used the two different patterns of silver knowing who in the family was to receive which setting each week. We never combined patterns for a person. That would be sacrilegious. The cloth napkins were folded just so.

Sunday dinners were always elaborate and perfectly prepared. My parents would be bustling in and out of the kitchen all afternoon basting the roast. Invariably, arguments would begin to surface between them on how done the roast was. My mother would begin preparing the rest of the dinner: relish tray, salad, vegetable, potatoes, rolls, roast, gravy, and dessert. My parents were both perfectionists and challenged each other throughout the meal preparation on seasoning, methods, and finesse.

We would finally gather after Mom called us to the table a number of times. Five children don't just materialize at the table at the first call. Dad would take his place at the head of the table and begin carving with all the plates in front of him. He would serve everything and pass it down to each child beginning with me and progressing up to the oldest, then my mother.

At some point, teasing and arguments would begin, and my mother would plead, "Let's all be harmonious." Sunday dinners never were. The dishes were perfectly prepared and everyone enjoyed them immensely except me. I would end up staring at a plate of meat, mashed potatoes, and vegetables long after everyone else had finished, stubbornly refusing to try even a bite. Usually, my brothers would perform great magic tricks by dragging their fingers slowly through the lit candles, while my mother was getting dessert in the kitchen, and Dad was clearing the plates.

After dinner was finished, we would all help put away food and finish clearing the table. My parents would clean up and wash the dishes. Even though we had a true luxury in those days, a built-in dishwasher, my father would don rubber gloves and sterilize each dish in hot sudsy water before it went in. We girls would make ourselves scarce. My brothers would be long gone, too.

The best memory was sitting together afterwards watching all our favorite Sunday evening television shows. All seven of us would gather in the small library in front of the television set, an odd contraption that had a six-inch screen magnified by a huge glass magnifier held in place in front of the screen by metal bars. We all had our special spots in the room. My father loved the *Jack Benny Show, Alfred Hitchcock Presents,* and we all looked forward to *I Love Lucy.* Dad would pass around the box of Fannie May® chocolates carefully hidden on his closet shelf and regularly raided by the six of us.

Sunday dinners were a mixture of tradition, tense moments, hysteria, laughter, and occasionally, some sadness, but most of all great food lost on no one except me. There was always going to be drama, and we did not hold back for any unsuspecting guest. The person who most keenly felt the highest level of embarrassment was I, as the youngest, and most sensitive in the family. I later learned that most of our guests, friends, and relatives loved eating at our house because of the built-in entertainment. As I have matured, I am able to look back on those wonderful dinners with great nostalgia and know that I would not have changed a moment. They helped shape who I am.

THE CHRISTMAS TREE

- by Kay Teeter

My heart sank as my mother said, "I think we won't get a Christmas tree this year."

How could we have Christmas without a tree? I saw the dismay on my brother Tommie's face. At the time, around 1960, I was about fourteen years old and he, about eight. Christmas held so few joys that such a loss felt devastating.

The three of us lived in a tiny upstairs apartment in an aging house in Springfield, Illinois. My mother put in strenuous hours working as a nurses' aide. (Her teaching certificate was out-of-date when the divorce occurred, so she had few options for going to work right away.) How was I to understand that her weariness, combined with very little money, made a Christmas tree seem like just one more burden? Without a car, even getting a tree home would not be easy. Our nearest relatives lived in Nebraska, so we fended for ourselves.

As I recall, Tom and I seldom pleaded for anything. One time that we did, however, was when my mother considered applying for an apartment in the housing project. I was mortified by the thought of such a "stigma," not truly understanding the difficulties of raising two kids on a limited income. My dismay, and Tom's, brought the housing project idea to an end, so we stayed in the same apartment, and my mother continued to struggle.

Like the thought of public housing, the prospect of not having a Christmas tree also affected me deeply. We didn't have family coming around for a tasty Christmas ham and fresh-baked pies. It was just the three of us, and I can't recall what our meal was like. Gifts were small and few in number, but my mother always tried to include something special. I still remember the pale-blue transistor radio, compact enough to hold in one hand. I don't know what my mother may have sacrificed to buy it. Perhaps some money from relatives paid the price. They sometimes helped financially, which may have added to the guilt my mother felt. She was the first in her family to be divorced and the

151

only sister of four to experience family difficulties. Her circumstances weighed heavily on her mind.

But Tom and I were children, and although we knew not to ask for much, some things are hard to give up. So we begged for a Christmas tree and said that we would even go get it ourselves. My mother relented, giving us the few precious dollars the tree would cost.

At twilight Tom and I set out for the nearest Christmas tree lot many blocks away on North Grand Avenue. We trudged through the glistening snow, chose a tree, and carried it home. We shared the weight between us, with me supporting the heavier trunk end and Tom, the prickly top. The walk seemed long as winter winds whipped our coats and stung our faces, but having a tree trumped any discomfort. In my mind's eye, I see two slight figures dimly bathed in the streetlights and stomping persistently through snowdrifts and icy patches, determined to hold on to something important for life's continuity.

Later, in the corner of the apartment, the simple decorations sparkled on the tree. Was it scraggly? Was it imperfect? Perhaps. But for me, it was the cherished Christmas tree never to be forgotten.

GEORGIA

- by Joy Rennich

I wrote her eulogy. I counted it an honor to know her. Georgia was my friend, sounding board, mother figure, prayer partner—all of these and more. We met by chance in 1986. I had the opportunity to go with my husband on a business trip, but needed someone to stay with our two sons, ages eleven and fifteen. Through a friend at church, we found Georgia. She was a reliable, warm person who agreed to stay for two weeks while my husband and I went to Europe. It was a good match.

Over the next five or six years we'd see each other at church, comment on how fast the boys were growing but, nothing more. When I became a deacon at church, Georgia was on my "Heart List." Each deacon was assigned a shut-in to watch over during a three-year term. By then Georgia was in a wheel chair and had moved in with her daughter and about fifteen cats. I was delighted to be assigned someone I knew.

My initial phone calls were pleasant, but when I asked to visit she said no. As time progressed she agreed to visits on her porch. She supplied the lemonade. I supplied the cookies. We found many subjects to talk about. Her life had been full—a devoted husband, four children, lots of golf, family vacations, good neighbors, and pleasant homes. Then the difficult times came. Her husband developed dementia. She and her daughter cared for him. Through escapes and near disasters they kept him at home until he died.

I usually iron each week, and as our friendship grew, ironing time was a good time to call Georgia. With the phone tucked under my chin, we covered many subjects—child rearing, travel, daughters-in-law, church, and life in general. Between serious talks we'd laugh at ourselves. Eventually, she began to trust me enough to let me visit inside her home. She knew I would not judge her. Luckily, I was not allergic to cats.

I was no longer her deacon. My term was up. It did not matter. Our friendship was sealed with laughter and joy in each other's company.

As her eyesight failed she memorized all the phone numbers of friends and family. They were her life line. She was an accountant by profession, and her mind was always quick and perceptive. She'd laugh with me as I sometimes could not even remember my kids' phone numbers.

At times we would go to a special activity at church or just for a drive. It was not easy, but she could stand and pivot from her wheel chair to the passenger seat of my car. One lovely day we went to Grand View Drive, opened all the car windows, and just enjoyed the breeze. She was always there to listen, talk, give advice when asked, and laugh.

When her oldest son died she lost some of her spark. The great granddaughter, whom she adored, brought smiles and laughter, but not as often. Her faith in an afterlife never wavered. She wanted to live, but when death came that would be all right. During our last couple of visits, we said what we had wanted to say.

She was eighty-nine when she died at home in her own bed the way she wanted it. It was a blessing to have known her.

THEN · AGAIN

A FEAST
OF THE SENSES

- by Linda Zears

Meals in my mother's kitchen were usually daily events of eating to keep hunger at bay. The kitchen felt hot, crowded, and messy. My mother's kitchen was a tiny, cramped, hurriedly constructed, post WWII nook with the bare essentials. A table that seated the five of us was jammed into a space that barely accommodated the table and needed chairs. Often, once we were all seated and dishes were passed, the food in them was overcooked, or odd looking, or funny smelling, or all three.

Most days, by the time we sat down to eat dinner, every available surface was filled with dishes Mom had used for preparation, opened canisters, empty cans, and utensils. The sink had vegetable peels and unidentifiable substances, sometimes floating in cloudy water poured from potatoes, usually clogging the strainer, and on more than one occasion, stopping up the slow and ancient drain. The stove would have spills burnt solidly to surfaces, pots and pans with things stuck in the bottoms, and more utensils with gooey things stuck to them, while they, in turn, were stuck to the stove.

My mother usually sat down looking harried, frustrated, and defeated. Not exactly something to look forward to with any anticipation. I suppose the cramped quarters and lack of equipment contributed to what seemed, even as a child, to be a constant state of chaos and disasters in my mother's kitchen. Mostly I think the fact that she was an only child who had lost her mother when she was seven years old and had no one to teach her about cooking created the setting for the daily scene.

Incredibly, however, there was one day out of the year when my mother became the mistress of the kitchen and produced a feast worthy of royalty. It was something that I always loved to be in the kitchen watching. On Thanksgiving, a transformation took place that defies explanation. On those days she would get up early and begin taking over the kitchen.

First, it seemed to make some sort of spatial difference for her to shove the table all the way against the wall and move her chair, the one on the near side of the table, completely out of the kitchen. Next she would begin to spread the ingredients and utensils she needed to make pies out on the table top. I loved watching her use that ancient, wooden rolling pin and dented flour sifter. She blended the ingredients for the pie crusts, adding the shortening, forming the dough balls and began to roll them out on sheets of waxed paper. After she had placed the pale, raw crusts into ancient pie pans, poured in the fillings, topped with the second crusts, she trimmed off the edges, and I watched filled with hopes that there would be scraps. Oh, the scraps were wonderful when she gathered them up, rolled them out again, spread butter on the newly formed creation, and sprinkled cinnamon and sugar on most of it. Often, she found a few nuts and raisins to add to the surface, and then rolled the whole thing up to be baked. Before long the air was filled with the wonderful, one-and-only aroma of this golden brown treat. And, then, it was ready to be cooled, sliced, and eaten, as soon as possible.

While the pumpkin, apple, and, usually, mincemeat pies were baking, and with their wonderful, spicy smells filling every corner of the house, my mother would clear off the table and ask me for help tearing up several loaves of stale white bread for making the stuffing. She would chop up onions and celery and sauté them in her cast iron skillet. In a huge, old pottery bowl she mixed the bread pieces with the celery, onions, sage, chicken broth, eggs, and oysters. She sometimes let me help with this, allowing me to squish the savory smelling ingredients between my fingers to get all the flavors thoroughly mixed. A different sort of spicy smell began to fill the air.

Next, came the wrestling of the turkey, which always looked to have been the biggest turkey the grocer could possibly have had. It would seem, at times, the turkey was going to win, but eventually, my mother would wrestle it into submission, getting it stuffed, trussed, and into the roasting pan. Out came the pies to cool on the cleaned off table, and in went the turkey to begin roasting and sending out its own delicious aroma.

Eventually, I would lose interest in what was going on in the kitchen and go my way to play or read a book. Hours later, we would be called for dinner. In between, my dad would end up in the kitchen, helping my mother remove the turkey, getting the stuffing out and into a dish, and carving the steaming slices of meat onto the platter. Other things had been going on in the kitchen during those hours.

We sat down to a kitchen filled with dishes brimming with fluffy mashed potatoes, brown sugar glazed sweet potatoes, giblet gravy, corn with a big dollop of butter on top, green beans with bacon, fragrant hot rolls, sparkling glass plates with olives, pickles, radishes, green onions, stuffed celery, cranberry sauce, a big bowl of oyster dressing, and, of course, a platter of steaming slices of turkey. We felt just like princes and princesses as we savored each bite. When we seemed stuffed beyond all endurance, then out came the pies! Two fingers of each, please! With lots of fresh whipped cream!

If the kitchen was cramped, we only felt cozy. If it was messy, we saw only a veritable feast. The food, instead of looking and tasting peculiar, was perfect. My mother would sit down and begin to serve with a calm, serene, almost regal countenance. And this was the meal that was anticipated all year. Not to mention the days of savory leftovers.

THE GARAGE ACROSS THE WAY

- by Eleanor Louise White

I live in the country, and when the weather permits, I sit on my big deck during the evening, which is located at the back of the house. It is my safe haven.

Problems are solved, memories relived, nature explored, and finally sweet peace.

After Ray passed away, all of the yard work and house repairs were left to me. I was in no way prepared to take on the job of yard master and handyman. Ross and Craig, son-in-law and grandson, were good to help at first, but all too soon, they were too busy with their own lives to help much. Because of their busy lives, I had to take a back seat when it came to receiving help. That does not set well with older people as we don't like waiting. Time is too precious.

I have never felt so alone in my life. I started noticing a man visiting at the neighbor's home. He was older, short, and had beautiful white hair. When I say neighbor, I mean people who live on the next acre. Every once in a while, he would wave to me if I was working in the yard or sitting on my deck.

Before long, he started mowing the neighbor's yard, as well as a small part of mine, where our yards connected. Curious, I climbed on my mower and bopped over to introduce myself. His name was Ron, and my neighbors were his sister and brother-in-law. He was going to stay with them, as he was selling his home because of a divorce settlement. He told me that he was 72 and retired. We visited a while, and I shared a little of my life with him. I thanked him for mowing a part of my yard, as I have almost two acres to mow, and he replied how much he loved mowing,

He took over the extra garage, in back of his sister's house, and made it a workshop. He would sit in the garage with the big door up and watch over the neighborhood. We don't have street lights where we live. At night, he would stay out there with the lights on, which became a source of comfort to me, when I would take my dogs out. I knew that all I would have to do is yell, and he would be there to help. I would sit on my deck in the evening and know a friend was close by. A few years passed, and we became good friends. When he would notice I needed help with something, he would be Johnny-on-the-spot to help. I soon realized that I was fortunate to have such a friend. He planted a big garden every summer, and I would often find fresh vegetables on my deck. His sister's yard became a place of beauty, as he planted flowers and landscaped. I was so envious.

One day, I got the bug I wanted a new tree to plant in the back yard to block my view of an ugly metal building that had been built on the acre next to me. So, Ron and I got into my Caddie, and took off to find me a blossom tree.

After much searching, we found one I liked, so I bought it. Guess what! The tree was too big for the trunk or back seat, so we had to open my sun roof, and insert the tree through the opening. We laughed all the way home, as I slowly crept the back roads. He took great pains planting that tree for me, and I anxiously awaited my first blooms.

That fall, he decided to visit a son, with whom he had a guarded relationship. Since the weather would not allow us to visit in the yard, he would call me about ten in the evening, just to talk. I sensed that his visit had not gone as well as he had expected, so I listened and tried to be the friend he needed. I felt his disappointment, and his unrest, with the way his life was going, and wanted so much to help him. We talked often.

One afternoon in November, about four o'clock, I was watching TV and feeling very restless. Two hours later, I received a call from another neighbor telling me that Ron had died. He had committed suicide in his beloved garage across the way.

I was devastated. What the hell was he thinking. Why would he do such a thing? I was so mad at him. Why didn't he call me, so we could talk his problems out? Then I started to blame myself for not realizing he was hurting so much.   To make matters worse, I soon learned that he tried to change his mind about dying, so he reached out to his sister, but she called her husband to come home from town instead of 911. By the time her husband got home, and he called 911, Ron was fading fast. They could not save him at the hospital. My friend was gone.

Now, a year and one half later, the garage sits dark. The little tree he planted died. The sister's yard is no longer a place of beauty.
Every time I sit on my deck, I have to see that garage across the way and remember Ron. Maybe soon my guilt, and hurt, will fade away.

TRIP TO LINDA'S - GUTSY

- by David F. Cook

Jean had lost her battle with melanoma, and now I am alone. All the estate matters were finished, and her final requests satisfied. Early in our marriage, we each bought life insurance so that if one should die, the surviving spouse would have some financial benefit.

My daughter Linda lived near Cedar Falls, Iowa; my son Victor lived in Bartlesville, Oklahoma; my mother and sister lived in Nebraska. I lived in Peoria, Illinois and was employed at the local tractor factory so my only free time was on weekends. A weekend trip to Cedar Falls by auto was practical, but travel to the other places wasn't.

I had completed flight training thirty years earlier but hadn't flown in the past ten. Why not take money from Jean's insurance settlement and buy an airplane? I could become current by taking several flight hours with an instructor. I contacted, Honest John, the used airplane salesman and was soon "kicking tires."

Here was a Cessna Cardinal airplane. It had a one hundred and eighty horsepower engine, four seats, and a controllable variable pitch propeller, certified for instrument flying, and many special radios and instruments. WOW! I could fly in the mountains or out over oceans, but the reality is that I will be flying over the flat land of Illinois. A sale was made, and soon I was able to view the world from my lofty position.

Weather for the coming weekend looked favorable, and a call to my daughter Linda gave me an invitation. On Saturday morning, I was at the airport, finished my preflight inspection, both tanks full of gasoline, clearance from the tower, and soon I was in the air and on my way. My flight altitude was 5500 feet, and I had just flown over the Moline VOR, which is a radio transmitter used for navigation. I was on the airway going towards Cedar Rapids, Iowa. I called the Cedar Rapids control tower and asked for permission to fly thru their control zone. I continued to monitor their radio and after several minutes I received this call.

"American Airlines 727 just departed Cedar Rapids on your airway at 5000 feet".

Soon a little black dot appeared on my wind shield. I watched as it grew bigger. Large turbine aircraft create a wake turbulence that could flip over a small plane. If I continue on this airway, the 727 will be 500 feet below me at our meeting.

I made a ninety degree turn to the left and held this heading for thirty seconds and then turned right to my original heading. This positioned me one mile from the airway center. As the 727 was passing I heard, "500 feet is not very much" and I replied, "Yes sir." The rest of the flight was noneventful. I landed at Cedar Falls, and we had a nice visit.

Sunday arrived, and soon it was time to leave and fly home. A weather report indicated low clouds so I filed an IFR (instrument flight rules) flight plan. I received my clearance from the control tower and soon was in the air at my assigned altitude of 5000 feet.

After passing Cedar Rapids the cloud ceiling had dropped and I was "in the soup" flying entirely by using instrument indications. The air was quiet, so the ride was smooth and piloting relatively easy. After passing Moline, there was a "hole in the clouds," and I saw I-74. This was a welcome sight, and I hoped that Peoria would be clear.

I contacted Peoria approach and was given clearance to start my decent from 5000 feet to 2000 feet which is the initial approach altitude. I was now at the outer marker, which is a radio signal and is located about 5 miles from the approach end of the runway. I continued on my present heading until I intercepted the localizer radio beam. This radio beam extends from the end of the runway at the same heading as is the runway. This localizer instrument has a vertical line indicator and is centered when on the runway heading. If I am left of the centerline, the vertical line will be left of its center or to the right if I am on the right side.

Also on this instrument is a horizontal line indicator which is the glide path indicator and this is the path to follow from pattern altitude to the runway end. If you are above the glide slope, the horizontal line will be above the instrument center. Similarly, if the line is below, you are low and must go up. The object is to keep both lines centered and cross at the indicator center.

I am past the outer marker, and the hair lines are moving towards their center. Just before they are centered, I must make corrections to stop their movements and remain centered on the indicator. At the same time I've reduced my power settings, lowered the nose, and I'm descending. Soon altitude indications were: 1500 feet, 1300, 1100, 1000.

I can't see the ground. Where is the runway? I've never done this by myself before. I always had a safety pilot, and when I removed my hood, the ground was clear and the sun was shining and the airport was visible.

I called the tower and reported that I was making a "missed approach." This is a procedure to climb to pattern altitude and fly a prescribed circle around the airport to the outer marker. When you receive clearance from the tower you can try again.

What should I do? I could go to Springfield, but it might not be clear. Another call from the tower indicated that a commuter plane had followed me and landed. They came out of the clouds at 600 feet. I had no choice; I had to land this airplane.

I got my clearance and started down. Soon I was at 1000 feet, 800, still in the clouds, 700, and at 600, I saw the rabbit lights. These are progressive blinking lights that lead you to the runway end. Now the runway lights are visible, and soon I'm on the ground.

Now when I fly, I must have at least a 1000 feet cloud base.

KAMAKURA, JAPAN

— by Mary L. Evans

In April, 1963, my roommate Florence and I went on a dream vacation—Hawaii, Japan, Hong Kong, and Bangkok; then back to Hong Kong, Hawaii, and then home. They were 4 of the most amazing, fun-filled, memorable weeks of my life.

Florence was the most organized person I have ever met, and from time to time, I still try very hard to emulate her. She had our itinerary all mapped out. All the places we wanted to see, with one exception, The Great Buddha at Kamakura. This would have to be a side trip made by 2 girls who knew no one in Japan, nor spoke a word of Japanese. Kamakura, is roughly 50 miles from Tokyo, and accessible by train.

Feeling very intrepid, we approached the concierge at the Imperial Hotel where we were staying and had him write the name of the train station in Japanese, on the back of a hotel card. Then we took our lives in our hands and hopped into a taxi and began our adventure. The strongest memory of all my Tokyo cab rides was one of overwhelming gratitude to God to have gotten me from point A to point B in one piece! The train station was very modern, as was the whole train system, and I am sure it is so today too.

We had no problem finding the ticket office and buying our 2 round-trip tickets to Kamakura. Finding the correct platform, was a little bit harder, but we managed. Japanese trains are electric and go exceptionally fast. They also do not stop long for people to depart or to board the train.

And the stations are all announced in Japanese. So once we got underway and realized what the situation was, we were looking at each other and laughing while wondering where we were going to end up, when this very nice young man approached us.

Although he was Japanese, he spoke excellent English, and asked us where we were going. When we told him that we were going to Kamakura, he said that was beyond where he was going. He then turned around and announced to everyone in the car, in Japanese, what our destination was and would they make sure that we got off the train safely and at the correct spot?

He got off the train at the next stop and from then on we were the only non-Japanese people on the train. I don't believe any of them spoke English, but they could not have been more dear. At every stop, which was announced in Japanese, they would smile at us and hold up 4 fingers, then 3 fingers at the next stop, until we arrived at Kamakura. There they got up and actually held the doors for us, and pointed us in the right direction. Fortunately, The Great Buddha was only about a block or two away, and being almost 47 feet high, was very visible.

The Great Buddha is made of bronze and is the second largest in Japan. It is also one where you can take photos. Most Buddhas being sacred, you are not allowed to photograph them. This one, even though it is in the Kotoku-in temple, still is very much in the open. You can go into it and see how it was made, which is very interesting. But the most lasting memory of that day, are the smiling, friendly Japanese faces on that train, holding up so many fingers indicating how many more stops we had to go. That kind of reception, you never forget.

THEN · AGAIN

LOOKING UP WHEN I HEAR A PLANE: MEMORIES BASED ON WHAT I HEARD

- by Sid Barnwart

One of the things I heard from my favorite spot in Arizona was a small plane passing overhead. Having earned my Private FAA Flying License in 1977, I almost always look up at a small plane and wonder about the pilot, the plane itself, and the journey that is underway.

That connection to my own flying and curiosity about the private flying of others led me to the Galesburg, Illinois airport over Labor Day weekend for several years in the late 1990s. The annual event was called the National Stearman Fly-In. Several hundred old Stearman planes would fly to Galesburg for fellowship and fun. They did formation flying. They did practice bombing runs to drop bags of flour on a target. They told stories about restoring these historic old planes. And they tolerated people like me who just came to talk and admire.

A Stearman design is a bi-wing plane. Built in the late 1910s and early 1920s, it had multiple uses. Some were used as military trainers to teach young aviators how to fly. Some were used to carry the first US Airmail; Charles Lindberg flew an airmail route in the Midwest. Some were used to perform stunts by barnstormers across the Midwest. They were slow, safe and reliable. They had open cockpits with the pilot sitting behind the passenger. The original design required someone to hand crank the propeller after the pilot was seated and had turned on the ignition. The consequences of not cranking the prop correctly were serious and severe. Not a job for the uninitiated.

As I walked through the parked rows of Stearmans early one Saturday morning, it became obvious that some were restored to original condition and design parameters. Others had been retrofitted with modern navigation, modern radios, and more powerful engines. The Stearman radial engines were unique and the people who seemed most fascinated by those radial engines were the people who owned motorcycles, with similar air-cooled heads.

I stopped to admire a beautiful red Stearman with the markings of the US Airmail Service on the side and struck up a conversation with the owner and pilot, Jim. He was an American Airlines pilot from Florida whose day job was to fly a large passenger jet from JFK to Paris. He said he had flown his 1929 Stearman up from Florida because: "It is way more fun than my day job, and you meet lots of great people along the way. Hey, would you like to fly with me down to Canton for breakfast today? I'm leaving in about 30 minutes." I jumped at the chance. As I climbed awkwardly into the front seat of the open cockpit, Jim asked if I saw the control stick between my legs and said pointedly, "Keep your legs spread wide because when I move the stick back here, the front stick moves in tandem. Understand?" I sure did.

As we taxied across the green grass wet with morning dew, it already felt like a real adventure. Jim turned the plane into the wind and opened up the throttle. We were quickly airborne at about 45 mph. Jim flew toward Canton at just above tree-top level, and we could hear children running outside exclaiming about the old red plane, saw farmers look up from their tractors and wave, and had time to take in the lush view of the early September countryside of a peaceful central Illinois morning.

In 20 minutes, we had landed at Canton and taxied up near the open hangar door where local pilots had prepared a huge breakfast for the Stearmans that had flown in just for that breakfast. We ate scrambled eggs, sausages, pancakes, and more.

It was fun to listen to the stories the pilots were telling. The pilot and passenger seated next to us at the picnic table for breakfast were both from Ohio. He also had a restored Stearman, but it had been used as a Navy Trainer, so was painted in military colors. His passenger was an air-to-air photographer, and before I had a chance to get a word in edgewise, plans were made for the two planes to fly back to Galesburg in formation. The other plane would lead and the photographer would take pictures of our plane flying over the farmland below.

Little did I realize how closely together these two planes would fly.

The lead plane flew several different courses, as well as above us, to provide the photographer with the best angle shots of our old red airmail plane. Jim was really milking this opportunity for all it was worth because, he said, good air-to-air photographers were a rare breed.

As we approached Galesburg, Jim and the pilot of the other Stearman started using hand signals to communicate because using a radio would have spoiled the experience! The two planes landed side by side, in tandem, on the grass at exactly the same spot. Just like professional show pilots. No big deal.

I thanked Jim profusely and offered to pay for fuel and breakfast, but he just said that it was good to be with someone who seemed to appreciate flying and the history of flying. I also gave my business card to the photographer and told him, that if it was possible, I would like to buy the series of shots he took of our plane. He said he would be in touch.

A couple of weeks later, a package of spectacular photos arrived in the mail. I called the photographer immediately to see how much I owed him. He said nothing, as long as he could have rights to the photographs that had my image. There I was in the front seat of every photo.

Today, one of those pictures is in the most prominent spot on my office desk at home. There I am in the front seat of a beautifully restored 1929 Stearman proudly wearing my Purdue baseball cap. My fellow Iowa State alums have never forgiven me for wearing the wrong hat.

Nor will I ever forget the generosity of that American Airlines pilot from Florida and the air-to-air photographer from Ohio. The serendipity of that early September Saturday morning is one of my favorite flying memories.

WARMTH, LIGHT AND CELEBRATION

- by Dottie Strickler

In the summer the sun is a warm blanket that covers everything, sometimes even smothering us with its heat. But sunshine in October is like a slim light saber whose warmth penetrates your body like a spicy jalapeño pepper pierces your tongue. And like the pepper it is a delicious heat in cool fall weather as is the tasty hot pepper in your mouth.

I sat on a bench in the woods to relish the sun's rays. Leaves were gently falling from black limbs of trees overhead. I gazed at the light showing through leaves of yellow, green, red, orange and brown. The light made them iridescent. I felt a cool breeze. The sun warmed my cold hands. What brought me to this sunlit place was the Mexican festival, Day of the Dead.

My son, twin grandchildren, and I went to a Day of the Dead celebration at his church. Though celebrating is not what we think of when remembering our loved ones, the Mexican tradition allows us to revel in the memory and honor the departed.

On the altar someone had carefully placed a blue vase of Calla lilies surrounded by yellow and orange marigolds and white candles. Above, sun shone through stained glass windows giving a welcome glow to the sanctuary. The music of a mariachi band playing guitar, harp, and trumpet filled the room. We sang Spanish songs that reminded us of the love and peace that comes with remembering. The minister spoke of how we can celebrate the lives of our family members who had died. Then he invited us to come and place a picture or other memento on the altar.

From my purse I took a photo of my Aunt Fannie Mae who had died in June. I bent down, and asked Zev and Zoe if they wanted to come with me. They took my hand, and we walked down the aisle, Zev on one side, Zoe on the other. They helped me light a slim tapered candle and place Aunt Fannie's photo on the table with the many framed pictures already there. I was proud to be seen with my beautiful four-year-old grandchildren. I said a prayer thanking God for my generous, kind and loving aunt. As we listened to the last notes of the mariachis, we left the sanctuary and headed for the social hall.

Delicious chili, Bread of the Dead, chips and salsa, pan dulce, and colorful sugar candies in the shape of skulls awaited on the tables. Zev and Zoe gobbled up the chips, salsa, and sugar skulls.

After lunch, Nate and the twins went to the playground while I slowly walked to a labyrinth, a few feet from the church's back door. Round stones formed the path to the center. I smelled the pungent brown wood chips as they sank into the wet ground under my shoes. Round and round I circled, finding peace. I thought of the quiet that was interrupted by the chirp of a cricket or tiny frog. I heard the crunch of shoes of another woman ahead of me. Silently, she let me pass. I heard the faint roar of cars whizzing by. A loud car radio reminded me of what a crisp fall day it was, and how people celebrate a beautiful day in many ways. Young people roll down the car windows and let the music spill onto the fresh air like the sun washes over the golden leaves around me.

I concentrated on the winding path, ignoring the tall oak trees above me in the woods. I felt the coolness of an early fall morning and the breeze as I stepped gingerly around the circle. I reached the middle. I changed direction to exit the circle. This day let me remember the past and appreciate the moments we have together in the present.

Is it like our lives? Paths we follow until we reach the center, finding who we are?

I returned to the bench and rested once again in the sun. It had been a day of warmth, light, and celebration.

THEN · AGAIN

THE AVENUE

- by Sonja Kerrihard

Mishawaka Avenue was a wonderful and exciting place to go. The avenue had a grocery store, bakery, hardware store, dime store, drug store, and a movie theater. I remember going to the avenue and visiting some of these places.

Going shopping with my grandparents was fun. We would go to the grocery store and Grandma would buy her groceries, Grandpa would probably go to the hardware store to purchase something that he needed. But the best part was when we would go to the bakery and Grandma would let me pick out something special just for myself. My favorite was cinnamon crisps. I would look at all the baked goods in the cases and always choose a cinnamon crisp. It always smelled so good at the bakery. I still like cinnamon crisps to this day.

On Sundays Grandpa and I would walk to the drugstore and buy a *Chicago Tribune*. We would walk back to my grandparents' house, and then he would read all of the comics to me. I remember the smell of the newspaper and looking for the comic section when we got home. I always wondered why Henry did not have a mouth. Henry was a comic strip character.

The drugstore had a soda fountain with tall round stools that I would twirl around on. After I had my appendix removed, the doctor wanted me to gain weight because I was so small. Mom would give me some money, and I would walk from my house on 25th Street to the drugstore and buy a milkshake. My mom thought that the milkshakes would help me gain some weight.

After school was out for the summer, the library always had a reading program for children. There was a bulletin board in the front of the library with a chart with the names of each child participating in the reading program. For every book a child read, he or she would receive a star. So every week I went to the library, returned the books I had read, picked out new ones, and put stars beside my name.

During the school year, the library had story hour on Saturday mornings. My sister and I would walk to the library to listen to the librarian read a book to the group of children who were there. My mom saved a picture that the *South Bend Tribune* took of a group of children at story hour. My sister and I are in the picture.

Bob and I would go to the River Park Movie Theater together sometimes. Bob and I lived on the same street. We would walk to the movie theater holding hands. I guess one might say that Bob was my very first boyfriend. We probably each had 25 cents for the movie and popcorn or a treat of our choice. Bob and I went all the way through grade school and high school together. At our high school reunions, Bob always had a hug for "his very first girlfriend."

Mishawaka Avenue has changed over the years. Most of these wonderful places are gone. But my memory of the wonderful and magical Mishawaka Avenue remains the same for me.

THEN · AGAIN

THE BABY
OF THE FAMILY

- by Kathleen L. Krippel

In a family with two children, they may be categorized as the oldest and the youngest. Even in a family of three, they may keep these categories with the addition of the middle child. But in a family with four children, generally the youngest is given the name "baby of the family." Alas this is what happened to me. I was born into a family with a Father, a Mother, two older sisters, Betty Ann - 9 years older, and Marietta (who we called Mimi) - 7 years older, and a brother Joe - 4 years older.

I am sure you have heard that the baby of the family is always spoiled. But I think the "baby of the family" gets a bum rap. First, the "baby" has to put up with a lot of unmerciful teasing from siblings.

I had my fair share. As many youngest children will attest to, there is the story of being adopted. When I was old enough to understand the meaning of adoption, my brother, Joe, told me, that I had been adopted. Of course I protested that this was a lie that he had again created to make me mad. On this occasion, he told me he had proof that I was adopted, and I asked to see this "proof." He said, "Just look at our family picture." Now back in the late forties, photographs were all black and white. So to make the photograph more appealing the photographer tinted the picture to make it look more "lifelike." My siblings all had blond hair. They took after my Mother. I took after my Father. We both had dark hair. However, in this family photo, I seemed to be tinted at least an extra shade darker then my siblings. Joe told me I had been adopted from a Mohawk Indian tribe. The proof was not only by the tint of my skin, but by all the dark hair that seemed to grow only on the top of my head. I suffered from his torment until one night while watching a TV program an adopted girl stated, "Her parents had chosen her, they wanted her, they didn't just have to accept what they got." I used that line on my brother. Then he confessed that he had lied, and I was his real sister. But then he asked me, if I ever thought, "why our parents didn't want any more kids after they had you."

This is the kind of stuff the "baby of the family" has to put up with from their siblings, and no amount of parent intervention can keep the baby from feeling this isn't true. I once made a comment to my sister, Mimi, that my head was extremely flat in the back. She, without missing a beat, said the reason for my flat head was, "You were so ugly as a baby, nobody wanted to pick you up, and so we just left you laying there in the crib." Now I knew I was a cute baby, there were a few pictures that testified to that, but the flat head and my sister's comment did make me wonder if Mom was just too busy with the others, that she didn't have time for me.

And that brings up another point. Did you ever notice that the oldest has lots of pictures and a baby book telling about everything they ever did as a baby. But with each new addition there are fewer pictures, and when it comes to the baby of the family, there's not even a book.

All children love to play games. And who doesn't want to win! But being the "baby" you never have a chance to win, because your older siblings have had more experience and know how to win, OR cheat. By the time the "baby" can win a game, nobody wants to play.

I remember a time when my two older siblings and I were going to play hide and seek in the house. I went to my oldest sister Betty, and asked for her help in finding a perfect hiding place. She put me up on the very top shelf of the hall closet and covered me up. Perfect! I thought. Joe came to closet several times, but never looked up, so he never found me. I was so happy! I was going to win! However, when they called out "Olly , Olly, Oxen Free," I couldn't get down. I yelled, but I guessed they couldn't hear me, OR was this all a sibling conspiracy to hide away the "baby" until she died of suffocation on the top shelf. Luckily, after what seemed like an eternity, my Dad came home, put his overcoat in the closet and found me sobbing away.

Gradually my siblings grew up and had better things to do then torment me. I had also learned not to react to their teasing. One wonders if the "baby of the family" ever loses that title. I don't know about others, but I believe I know when I lost the title for good. A time when miracle of miracles, I felt like an equal and respected member of our family. But that is another story.

———————————

SMELL

- by Brooks McDaniel

Next to music, aromas are the most mystical, most memory-producing of our connections to our experiences. Hence incense, hence perfume.

On a hot, quiet Saturday in July, I was filling up my car with gas at Robbie's when I smelled something I hadn't smelled in a long time. The mechanic was sitting in a chair in front of the automotive bay, smoking a pipe. I hadn't seen anyone smoke a pipe since my son's father-in-law in England quit about six years ago.

I smoked a pipe for twenty years. My first pipe and tobacco I bought in the Bradley bookstore, September, 1957. I was just eighteen. The stereotype college man, "cool with a pipe, reflective, mature," maybe!? The tobacco was Brush Creek. It had latakia whose little black flecks gave off the smell of a wood fire—ah, campfires, fireplaces, romance. I hallucinated that smell. Even when I wasn't smoking, I'd smell it. Could have been in my clothes, or hair, or all in my head.

That was the beginning. I switched to Cherry Blend. One night with several guys from the fraternity, I went to Collin's Corner to hear a rhythm and blues quintet headed by Jimmy B. We were slumming in that black and tan dive, digging the jazz. I wasn't drinking beer, probably soda, but after about an hour, I had to go to the john. I was smoking Cherry Blend. Standing next to me at the urinals, an older black man said, "Hey Man, that's some sweet smellin' stuff. Whadda you got?" Flummoxed and fearful, I blurted out, "It's just Cherry Blend tobacco." He said, "Oh...so, you don't smoke nothin' wroooong?"

After Bradley, we moved to Chicago where I went to McCormick Seminary and went right on smoking my pipes and collecting them. To my delight and amazement, down on Wabash in the loop, was Iwan Ries & Company. The place was like a pipe museum: carved Meerschaums, Sherlock Holmes type. Church wardens—the long stemmed clays you could rent in pubs 150 years ago. There were corncobs, cherry woods with the bark still on, imported briars, and elegant and expensive crafted pipes of every size, shape, and price. I was in heaven. The place was permeated with sacred incense. They tailor-made half a dozen blends of tobacco, the best, most famous was "3 Star Blue." I must confess, all pipe tobacco smells better than it tastes.

After puffing my way through seminary, I became a Pastor of the Marquette Heights Presbyterian Church. I discovered a useful pastoral application. When counseling, you could wait out a reluctant counselee in silence as you tapped-out the ashes, reloaded, and relighted.

But one night after a long day as I was drifting off into twilight sleep, half-dreaming, I saw myself laid out in the operating room, on the gurney, with a huge dome-light above me and the surgeon was removing my voice box. I was a fast-puffer and every night my tongue would be roasted and my throat burning. Slow-learner, but the thought occurred to me: "I make my living talking. This is really a dumb thing to do."

I didn't quit then. I went on to teach at Illinois Central College and kept on puffing. All the while, supporting my growing family, making my living, talking. By this time, I was smoking a tobacco called "Revelation." It was cheap and had some resonance with my occupation.

By the time my son was eight and my daughter, six, they were getting strong propaganda in school, against smoking. I would be in my office, grading papers at home, smoking my pipe, with the door closed. My son would burst into the room and say, "Dad! Dad, you're killing yourself!"

That was when I quit. I don't miss it. But, seeing the mechanic at Robbie's with his pipe, there was just a whiff of the incense of reminiscence.

THEN · AGAIN

THE DESINARE
(MEAL, IN ITALIAN)

- by Nancy E. Dugard

In September 2010, Ed and I celebrated our fiftieth wedding anniversary. In honor of this milestone, we took a European trip. A portion of this trip was spent in Italy. When in Italy, we always spend a couple of days in Calascio, the town where my mother-in-law was born. Calascio is located on a mountain range in the Abruzzi region, about two hours northeast of Rome toward the Adriatic Sea.

A friend of ours from Chicago, Carl Marinacci, owns a house there. He usually visits Calascio and stays for an extended period of time in the late summer and early fall.

Although we typically stay with Carl, this time he had guests visiting, so we stayed in a bed-and-breakfast nearby. Our plans were made prior to our arrival, and on this particular Sunday evening, Carl had suggested we have dinner in San Stefano, five miles from Calascio.

The evening began with cocktails at his house. When it was time to leave for dinner in San Stefano, Carl changed his mind. He said, "Let's eat at Da Clara," which is a restaurant right down a stone walkway from his place. As that was fine with us, we walked with Carl and his friends down to the Da Clara restaurant.

We entered in the side door and from this angle we could not see the main dining room. So, when we walked into the dining room, Ed and I were in total shock. There were balloons, crepe paper, and streamers everywhere! Carl said, "Did you look up?" There was a huge banner made out of oil cloth hanging on the wall. It measured three and a half feet tall by seven and a half feet wide. Printed on it was our wedding picture with greetings written in Italian. The beautiful gold lettering read:

"Buon Anniversarioper il 50 anno di matrimonio di Nancy ed Edwardo Con tanto amore, i figli i Calascini Calascio, Setembre 2010"

Translation: "Happy Anniversary for the fiftieth year of matrimony with a lot of love, the children of Calascini. Calascio, September 2010"

The owner of the restaurant and staff were in line waiting to greet us and wish us a happy anniversary with the hope of many more happy years to come. As this restaurant is usually closed on Sundays, the owner had opened just for us and a special meal prepared for the party. At ninety-three years of age, the owner had stopped working, but came in to help his daughter prepare a feast for us. Of course, all conversation was in Italian. Thank God Carl speaks Italian!

As a side note, it had been a special summer for Da Clara's restaurant. George Clooney was filming *The American* a few miles away, and he ate most of his meals there. Another interesting fact, Da Clara's building was originally a convent.

What a wonderful celebration! The meal was delicious, the wine superb, and the company great. We took lots of pictures, and laughed and reminisced about our lives.

Now how did all of this come about? How did Carl know it was our fiftieth anniversary? Mystery solved. Our children had been discussing our anniversary, and this was one of their brilliant ideas. Our youngest son, Greg, planned it and called Carl to have him set it up. The Mayor of Calascio was a friend of Greg's and while he was invited to the dinner, he regretfully could not attend. Our daughter, Janet found our wedding picture and had it scanned to Carl who ordered the banner and arranged everything. Although Carl wanted to write the banner in English, Greg said absolutely not. It had to be written in Italian.

Of course, Ed and I had to buy an extra suitcase in order to bring the banner home.

THEN · AGAIN

BOWLING LESSONS

- by Susan K. Camacho

My very unhappy looking 7-year-old came through the back door, passed through the kitchen where I was doing dishes, and threw his sturdy, little body face down on the couch in the family room. "Well, hello to you, too, Benjie," I said baffled. "Did you not have fun at the scout meeting? Where's Dad?"

Just then, Ben came in seemingly oblivious to an obvious problem. "Did something happen at the meeting?" I asked my husband with a nod to our pouting son.

"Dad's on call next Saturday, and won't be home till late, so that means I can't be in the Father/Son Bowling Tournament, and I am mad, and I DON"T CARE!" came the crescendo of angry words from my first-born son.

There was only one logical solution to the drama. I picked up my darling little towhead and announced that I would be subbing for Dad, and that Benjie and Mom would be rolling some balls, and knocking down some pins next Saturday.

"Nooooooo," screamed my wiggling boy. "A Mom can't be in the Father/Son Bowling Tournament!"

It took a week of persuasive convincing, but eventually, the desire to be part of the action won out. Saturday came around, and it seemed that it was Mom or nothing. Head down, ashamed to look anyone in the eye, Benjie sulkily walked beside me to our assigned lane.

Three dad-looking guys in t-shirts and jeans stopped their friendly exchange and stared.

"Where's your dad, Benjie?" Mr. Take Charge said.

"He can't come; my mom is going to bowl with me," my embarrassed son mumbled.

I offered tokens of friendship, a big smile and a handshake, trying to prove that I was here to have fun and be a team player. I really couldn't help being a girl, a very pixyish looking girl, with a cutesy little name.

The three chauvinists were not having any of it. No interest in the smile; stuck their hands in their pockets in refusal of the handshake.

"Well, then, guess you're up first, Soooooozaaaaaay." Mr. Dagger Looks announced.

I strolled to the ball holder, cooled my palm in front of the little grate, picked up the ball I had chosen for its lightness, and turned my back to the bowling bullies. I took a big, cleansing breath and gave the pins a good, hard look. The raucous sounds of hyped up boys, authoritative dads, and wooden pins crashing loudly on the hard floor, faded away.

I started my three-step approach with my right foot, set my chin level, and stared at the center point in the painted arrow in front of me. I let my ball swing down close to my side and then slightly up in the air behind me as my body curled over. With my knees bent, I curtsied and swung the ball through with ease to silently touch the floor and start to roll down the alley, passing the intended triangle barely to the right of the point. I stayed slightly bent as I continued my ball hypnosis but squared my narrow shoulders as the ball smacked just to the right of the kingpin, and the rest of the bottlenecked soldiers fell quickly in surrender.

The scouts behind me were cheering as I turned around to face the Dour Dads. Mr. Bland felt his comment, "Beginners luck," was necessary.

"Bring it on, sukkahs; I'm just warmin' up. Don't mess with the Momma!" my gaze said.

Well, that afternoon, the big boys couldn't get on a roll, and I couldn't get off mine. After my third strike in a row, the Dubious Dads started coming around. The stale air seemed to refresh as the other teams took notice of what was happening in our lane.

My score was close to 200 that day. Benjie and I got big hugs and were sent home with the shiny gold-plated team trophy. I learned a lot that day, and hopefully, so did my son.

A MEAL
TO REMEMBER

by Susan Rigg Grandt

Do you like pizza as much as I do? Chicago is known for great pizza and many people are familiar with the deep dish pies popular on the North Side. But where I grew up on the South Side, the very best pizza was the thin crust perfected by Vito and Nick at their restaurant on South 84th Street and Pulaski Road. That was where I had an especially memorable meal with my parents in January, 1969.

I was home on semester break from the University of Illinois at Urbana-Champaign. At 20 years old I was a senior looking forward to graduating that spring and as far as my parents knew, committed to being single. I had made it through high school and college without any serious boyfriend and had no boyfriend then, to their knowledge. Imagine their surprise when, while we were waiting for our pizza that night, I announced that I was going to get married!

That might have been the only time ever when my parents were both struck speechless. When they finally did speak it was to ask me WHO I planned to marry.

"Terry," was my answer.

Then they asked, "WHO IS HE?"

"Remember the guy you met once last fall at that get-together at my roommate's parents' house? That guy," I replied.

Flash forward to 1979. Terry and I had been married for 10 years then and had 2 sons of our own. My Dad and I were reflecting on that night at Vito and Nick's when I had told him I was getting married. At my ripe old age of 30, I wondered what he had thought of my 20-year-old decision to marry someone I had only known for a few months, and he didn't know at all.

He said he figured by age 20 I was going to do what I wanted anyway, so there was no sense in him objecting. Besides, he had taught me to use good judgement in my choices over the years, so he trusted that this choice was the right one for me.

I don't remember what toppings we chose for our pizza that night.

Choosing a pizza isn't so important. Choosing a spouse is very important. As of August, 2014 Terry and I were married for 45 years, so I must have made the right choice!

———————————

SOMETHING I LIKE TO DO: ENTERTAINING DINNER GUESTS

by Jackie Krag

As a child it was always exciting when Mother prepared a luncheon or dinner party for friends. Wonderful aromas of special things she would serve like made-from-scratch Parker House rolls drifted from the kitchen. Fresh cut flowers were in the center of the dining room table. On the white linen table cloth, with folded napkins at each place, were the Lenox™ china decorated with pretty flowers, polished King Edward sterling, and sparkling glassware. The guests arrived in dressy clothes. They spent a long time at the dining room or card tables, laughing and chattering. Afterwards we children were delighted to have some of the left-over "company food," especially the tasty rolls, for supper.

For years I had seen how easily Mother entertained guests. In the years to come, I enjoyed using the beautiful wedding gifts that we received to entertain our family and friends. As young, married parents, entertaining in Peoria was pretty simple as I served food that I could easily prepare. When we moved to Sweden [and Casablanca], there were many opportunities to entertain American friends, as well as new friends and customers. But it was not always easy.

[One year, while we lived in Sweden,] I decided to invite 12 for Saturday Thanksgiving dinner. I had seen and even helped Mother prepare many Thanksgiving dinners. In 1956, turkey was a delicacy in Sweden that could be ordered only from Nordquist's, the food purveyor to the Royal Family. Most of the American foods that I would need, I could also purchase there. However, when I realized that enough small cans of Sand W cranberries would cost about as much as the turkey, the clerk introduced me to the Swedish lingonberries.

Livsmedals (grocery stores) closed at 3:00 on Saturday afternoon and opened at 8:00 on Monday morning. Having planned and worked on the meal during the week and going into Stockholm to pick up the turkey, I was ready to put it in my trusty GE electric roaster on Saturday afternoon; the oven was too small. By 4:30 there was an aroma of fish in my house. Fish was never on my shopping lists. I had all the food for my guests, but I did not have a substitute for the turkey. In a panic, I called my mentor and dinner guest to see if she knew of any livesmedal where I could buy meat. She laughed and said not to worry, "The Swedes don't have enough corn to feed to their livestock, so they feed it fish. The odor will disappear." By the time the guests arrived at 7:00, the fish odor was gone. We enjoyed the turkey dinner and laughed a lot, even though I didn't tell them of my near miss.

Between our assignments in Stockholm and Casablanca, we were on our biannual home leave and stayed with my parents. At the dinner table one evening my father said a client was going on a cruise of the Mediterranean on the U.S.S. *Constitution* with friends in September. Their first port of call was Casablanca. We had enjoyed entertaining visitors who came to Sweden, and I told him to please invite her to have dinner with us in Casablanca.

[In Casablanca] almost all of the representatives of foreign governments or companies had house boys. I was so blessed to have Hassan, a young Moroccan man in his early twenties. As a young boy, he had worked for and been trained by a French lady who had taken him to France for three years. He had just returned to Morocco, married Aisha, a very young girl from the "bled" (country), and needed a job. Of course, he spoke Arabic and French but said only "Hello" and "Thank you" in English. He smiled a lot, was very pleasant, and enjoyed our three children.

Eager to learn some French, I had gone to three Berlitz® classes before the U.S.S. *Constitution* came into port in Casablanca. Through my French-speaking neighbor, Hassan knew I was expecting dinner guests. He could hardly wait to show me his serving skills. [On the day our visitors arrived] I saw the ship on the horizon, [and Hassan and I went to the dock.]

We had been in Casablanca only three weeks. I had no idea how to get to the harbor, [but Hassan was my navigator.] With lots of "Madam" and hand motions, we arrived at the dock as the passengers were ready to disembark. I knew my father's client only by name as she was the organist in a large Peoria church. I'm not sure how I selected her, but after I asked if she were "Miss Bone from Peoria," we became immediate friends. Then, I asked if her traveling companion would like to join us. Imagine my surprise when her friend was Miss Burns, my seventh and eighth grade home economics teacher at Whittier School, and an acquaintance of my mother.

We had such a good time chatting through dinner and enjoying the view. Before long I noticed that the water glasses were almost empty. I was ready to practice my newly acquired French on Hassan when he entered the dining room. "Dorme bien, Hassan," I said. He had a most peculiar expression, lowered his eyes and head, and replied, "Oui, Madam." But he just stood there, so I repeated, "Dorme bien, Hassan." He replied "Oui, Madam," but he didn't move a muscle.

Miss Burns came to his rescue —and—mine when she asked, "Jackie, what is it you would like for him to do?" I told her that I would like Hassan to fill the water glasses. She started to laugh as she spoke in French to him and, then, to tell me that I had told him to go to bed. We all had a very good laugh over that, and the evening continued until it was time for Hassan to guide us back to the ship. That was my first dinner party in Casablanca and the beginning of many laughs with Hassan.

CRICKET'S

- by Jim Feurer

Cricket's, in rural Wisconsin, is one of the best people-watching places I have experienced since Sara's Road House on Route 6. My journalist friend Phil, a controversial column writer for the local newspaper would love Cricket's. It has Phil written all over it. He would love the people and all the artifacts that adorn all the walls. And of course, the beer.

On display are mounted: huge pike, northern pike, walleye, and muskie, small and large mouth bass, several mounted heads of deer, moose, you name it. Besides the huge black bear, there are other full-size wildlife creatures such as, wolves, fox, raccoon, and badger placed about the bar room.

Old and new beer signs of all kinds clutter all the walls. There are dart games, a juke box, pool table, even a toy-retrieving machine with a little crane. And it even works. Phil would also marvel at the tattered swiveling bar chairs and tore up padded bar once repaired with almost matching duct tape.

Next to the bear is a huge bulletin board advertising personal items for sale and public notices telling of past and coming events. Some of the walls are adorned with the same. Business cards of all kinds are also posted with push pins and many more are in a jar for drawings.

I will say, the place is clean. Even the modest rest rooms are spotless. Believe it or not, bless Chris and John's hearts, when you dry your hands there is not some damn noisy antiquated hand blower or just a roll of paper towels. Cricket's restrooms have modern, motion-automated towel machines! Cricket's is all trumped with unreal, to-die-for good food, and super friendly owners, staff, and patrons. Even with all the drinking, I never have heard a cross word in Cricket's. Mostly laughing or yelling at the ref on TV during a Green Bay game.

The bartenders and bar maids are amazing entertainment. Most are Native American men and women. At least half the drinks are mixes. Some I never heard of. Watching those drinks being fixed and served, nonstop, is like watching an alcohol ballet. Besides hard liquor and wine, there is beer in cans, bottles, and several draft choices. And of course soft drinks.

One of my favorite beers, my son in law Doug and daughter Jackie share, is draft Rolling Rock.® It is served in genuine green Rolling Rock® 16 oz. jars. Yes we have a Rolling Rock® jar at our cabin—compliments of Chris—a token of his appreciation of our good patronage. A good Friday night at Cricket's with our family will net a tab of well over $100 for food and drinks!

I look forward to Cricket's above all other establishments in Wisconsin. Cricket's has become our north country family tradition. In fact June 5th, 2015, my wife Linda and I, along with daughter Jackie and our son-in-law Doug, celebrated our 50th wedding anniversary with Friday night fish at Cricket's.

The fish: Wow! All you can eat. $9.95 broiled or deep fried with Cricket's special beer batter to swoon over!

CONVERSATIONS WITH STEPHIE

by Lucy McCrea

All grandparents have these stories to tell and all of us all think they are unique and wondrous stories.

Stephanie, my first grandchild, was twenty-six last month. It is amazing to me how fast times go by. Wasn't it just last week that she was learning new words? I don't have many memories of my own children when they were learning to talk. Probably because I had little time to sit and observe in those days. But I have enjoyed those times with my grandchildren.

When Stephie heard a new word, she would duck her head and whisper it over and over to herself. The first time I noticed this was when we saw a squirrel on television. I said it was called a squirrel, and she bent her head, and I heard her whispering "curl, curl, curl."

Shortly after that, in October, she was at my apartment when I brought out the Halloween decorations. She pointed to a ceramic jack-o-lantern my mother had made and looked at me. I showed her a picture of a pumpkin and explained what you did to make it into a jack-o-lantern. Her grandfather, my daughter-in-law's dad, was astonished when she saw a pumpkin at their house and asked if he was going to make it into a jack-o-lantern and explained how he could do that.

One morning I had been driving around on an errand with her in the car. She kept asking a question: "Hawaiian Go?" At least that was what I heard. She asked it at least a half dozen times, and I still didn't understand. Finally she said, "Kitty go Me-ow. Doggie go Wuf. Hawaiian go?"

At last I understood. We had stopped at my younger son's office, and he had given her a stuffed lion that was a symbol of the company he worked for. She wanted to know how lion go? I did my best to sound like the MGM lion for her. (I wish I had written this down at the time, so I knew exactly what age she was when this happened.)

A little later she got into storytelling, and she was quite imaginative. She told us about Rainbow Kitty, and the mice who lived in the pocket of her raincoat, and the dog who liked to ride the rocking horse. And she told about the owls who lived in her closet in the old house and stayed back there when Stephie and her family moved. A couple of months later she reported that they suddenly appeared in her bedroom closet at the new house. Once I must have seemed to take her too seriously, so she said "It's pretend, you know."

My favorite conversation with Stephie took place in early spring when she was four years old. We were driving down Forest Park Hill toward the Nature Center. The Nature Center wasn't our destination this time, but we had visited there a number of times. Stephie especially liked to look at the snakes, and she was allowed to take them out and hold them, something not every child her age would enjoy.

We had been there the previous fall when they advertised a story-teller who would tell stories for Halloween. So we went. Stephie was the only child there to listen, but the storyteller, a very pleasant older women, carried on and told a number of stories about the gnomes who lived there and did good deeds, such as finding a Girl Scout who had been lost back in the days when that place was a Girl Scout camp.

After all of the warm stories about the gnomes, the storyteller told about the terrible trolls who lived under a bridge and would grab children and throw them in a kettle of boiling water to cook them for lunch. I was stunned. How would Stephie react to a scary story like that? I didn't say anything about it on the way home and neither did she. She seemed happy and cheerful. Apparently those scary trolls hadn't bothered her.

This day, driving down the hill, I remarked: "We should go visit the Nature Center again some time. We haven't been there since last fall when we heard the stories about the gnomes."

"Yeah, and the trolls," she said in a tone of voice that told me I had been wrong; she had been scared by that troll story.

"There aren't really any trolls," I said. "They are just something to pretend about, to scare ourselves for fun. Something that just isn't real. Like the bogeyman."

"Yeah," she said "and the Easter Bunny."

Uh oh! I didn't want to have this conversation. I didn't want to talk about the reality of the Easter Bunny. Her parents, especially her mother, wouldn't be happy if I exploded that myth. So, I did the best I could. "Oh, really. I never saw the Easter Bunny, but I always assumed there was one."

"No, I'll tell you what it is. It's just a regular rabbit and it brings a chicken."

"Oh, of course. To lay the eggs," I say.

There was a long pause.

"I think there must be an artist."

"I see. To color the eggs before you wake up."

"Yeah."

Another long pause.

"I think they bring a hair dryer."

HOUSE ON FIRE

by Nancy A. Huber

There was no warning. The day turned from a warm cheerful one to a dark menacing black sky as black as coal. Lighting and thunder joined in the hellish dance. Rain beat down hard and loud. Never in my young years of life did I ever see such a violent day.

The lights were gone. "Albert, did you turn out the lights?" Albert was my teenage cousin, reading his comic book in the other room.

"NO," he yelled back. My kid brother, Ernie, was in the same room, but I knew Ernie wouldn't turn out the lights. The upstairs was all lit up, so I dashed upstairs. At the top of the stairs, I saw live blazing wires racing down the grassy field. The wires passed over the top of the front porch catching the old wood house on fire.

Down the stairs I flew calling to Ernie, "Get out of the house, Ernie! The house is on fire!"

Ernie was small but very fast. He ran out the front door, and I was right behind him. Leaving the porch he went a short distance, and his body was lit up like a Christmas tree. I couldn't think, I just knew I had to get Ernie out of danger. I grabbed his hand and now the both of us were victims. It lasted only seconds, but it felt like eternity. It threw us back to the front of the porch. We were in a daze and confused. We couldn't go out the front way, and we couldn't return to the house on fire.

Many neighbors lined the road in the rain and dark shouting something to us. I couldn't understand their frantic voices. One brave man tried to jump the fence to come to our aid, but the current threw him back.

Another brave teenager came as close as he could, and I understood his high pitched voice. "Go through the house and out the back yard. There are no wires in the back yard." We had no choice but to follow his orders.

On our way through the house, we passed my calm cousin, Albert. Ernie and I were shook up but not so was Albert. He let us lead the way, and when he felt it was safe, he would follow.

Out of the back door, and there a neighbor met us with flashlights and took us to her home seating us in front of her coal-burning stove. Ernie and I tried to stop shaking, but Albert found the soft seat, slowly reached in his back pocket pulling out the comic book he was reading, and continued reading when he was interrupted.

The rain drowned out the flames and the house was safe. However the black scorching marks at the top of the porch remain as a permanent reminder of that night. It took years before that house was torn down.

THEN · AGAIN

WHAT I KNOW
FOR SURE

- by Barb Benner

There's an old adage that the only certainty in life is that of death and taxes. While that is believed by most, it is debated by politicians on the part of taxes. The general population still agrees on the death part.

There's one thing I know for sure. I'm convinced this to be true, and I try to follow my life behaviors in this daily philosophy. I believe that you cannot survive this life without a sense of humor.

We live in tumultuous times, with levels of stress, discord, unrest, and controversy. It is an absolute that there has to be a break, a relief, and I feel that sense of rescue comes through humor. Whether you laugh, giggle, or snicker, the very body exercise gives an immediate re-action. If we choose to laugh at our self, tell a comical story, repeat a joke, or even quote an email of whimsy, we somehow feel better.

Any method or avenue of communication will work. I find I can make myself feel better by recall of something that was funny to me. I don't think my particular life has been funny; on the contrary, it has been a rather serious one. But, have you noticed that a belly laugh, a chuckle, or even a snort in the name of humor is contagious?

I'll give you a simple example from a life experience that happened in 1977. I was on an airplane, aisle seat of a mid-section of a large aircraft. These were days when there was a smoking section on the seating charts, and you were served full meals by busy stewardesses. I was the "odd man out" in our group of three, so the two other gals sat by the window. I was able to be next to them with the aisle in between.

It had been a quiet uneventful flight. Lunch time came, and we were all served a fine meal, and we had real dishes with real silverware, even if it was the commercial quality with the airline logo on it. All went well, and the noise of the cart came from behind as the stewardess was in the process of cleaning up and picking up the dinnerware trays.

She reached across me to obtain the tray from the man next to me. As she raised the tray over our heads, all of a sudden, his knife slid right off the tray and onto the lady's head in front of me. The knife landed perfectly flat on the lady's "shelf" hairdo.

I know I was shocked, but my immediate reaction was to put my hand over my mouth to choke the laughter that was begging to just jump out. The stewardess never flinched, never dropped pace. She just reached onto the woman's hairdo, said "excuse me ma'am," and promptly picked the knife up and put it with her cart items.

My eyes began to water with my cinched in yells of laughter, and I rolled my eyes about 45 degrees to my right to see if the gentleman next to me had seen what happened. When our eyes met, that was it. We both laughed out loud. The lady involved never knew what had actually landed on her "shelf," and she was not cognizant of what we had seen.

This calm, quiet Canadian shirt-and-tie started up a conversation, and after we calmed our giggles, had a lovely visit the rest of the flight. That had been just one of those fluke accidents that caused no harm, but gave two of us a moment to share and probably remember for years yet to come.

Some folks have a theory that it is better to laugh than cry. While I tend to agree with that thought, I also know for sure that a moment of laughter, or operation of the humor machine, can save us from the frustration of many a moment. I know for sure that sometimes we need to go with the flow and relish the moment, the whimsy, or the comical experience. You can be short or tall, skinny or not, young or chronologically gifted, but humor is a universal antidote. Whether it be droll, silly, or downright hilarious, a sense of humor is medicine that we can all afford.

SENSES — SMELL: FRESH CUT HAY

- by Bill Ligon

It was the summer of 1962, and I had just completed my ROTC (Reserved Officers Training Corp) summer camp in Virginia. Someone had a car, and five of us and our gear were crammed into it on our way home. They also had a relative that lived on a farm in the Pennsylvania Dutch area, and we were invited to stop for dinner.

The smell of fresh cut hay has stayed with me, as well as the wonderful home cooked meal that we were provided by this welcoming family. That smell brings back memories of the summer camp experience and my beginning military journey. I signed up for ROTC primarily to get some spending money; I was on a very limited budget as I attended college. At the time I had no idea that it would ultimately lead me to Vietnam in 1965-66.

The summer camp was to give us future officers a taste of the basic training new inductees had to go through. It was the first time I had been out of Illinois; my home was just east of St. Louis, and eastern Missouri was where I attended the University of Missouri at Rolla studying Civil Engineering. I should have been assigned to the combat engineers (summer camp was at Ft. Leonard Wood, Missouri), but because of my extreme nearsightedness was assigned to Ordnance. This turned out to be a positive as the ordnance summer camp was to take me to Ft. Belvoir, Virginia (just south of Washington, D.C.), Ft. Lee, Virginia (just north of Washington, D.C.), and Aberdeen Proving Ground (on the north shore of the Chesapeake Bay in Maryland). When I entered the Army for real in the fall of 1964, I was assigned to Aberdeen Proving Ground for basic officer's training.

One of the things I really enjoyed in all my military experiences was the amazing array of characters I met and worked with. It started with this summer camp. I had my first exposure to guys from the Deep South. We had cadets from Georgia Tech who were from Georgia and the Carolinas and indeed had a very deep southern drawl. They were great guys though, and I enjoyed getting to know them. We had a career Captain as our company commander and a career Staff Sargent to oversee our unit (some would say to also harass us—the army's way to introduce you to the military). We had some issues with our overzealous captain who his boss informed us was acting like he did because he was going through a divorce.

One of the experiences I remember was spending a week at Ft. Lee in the woods, in tents, shaving out of our helmets with cold water, and generally getting the idea that being in the field during combat was no picnic. We were also introduced to K rations (left over from WWII). There is nothing like eating cold beans and wieners from a can. Another was doing pull-ups while waiting in line to eat, and I am proud to say I could do the second most pull-ups (around 20 as I remember) in our company. The guy who could do the most was a wrestler from Purdue.

The captain liked to yell at us when he felt we were moving too slowly. One time I was acting platoon officer as we were marching to lunch. He thought we should be doing double time and came running up yelling. We had a guy who did great "Jody Calls," and I asked him to do so (we really did sound great); the captain pulling up so short he almost fell over. Having pledged a fraternity, the harassment really did not bother me, and I certainly did not take it personally.

Overall I have fond memories of this experience and must have done well as I was made a Colonel in our ROTC unit at school my senior year. The smell of the fresh cut hay to this day reminds me of my ROTC summer camp experience.

THEN · AGAIN

MY HERO

- by Sue Mullen

My dad has always been my hero. He was a World War II hero, a flight engineer on a B29, and a POW in Russia (our ally) for eight months. He was awarded a POW medal in 1992. (Prior to that time, his mission was a "secret.") As a war hero, he and his wife were eligible to be buried in Arlington National Cemetery. That is remarkable all by itself.

As a young child, my dad moved us around in search of a good job after the war. Indianapolis, Indiana, Homewood, Illinois (he was recalled to serve in the Air Force during the Korean War), Bridgeport, Connecticut, Cincinnati, Ohio, Moline, Illinois, and finally Peoria. He always wanted to better himself and his family's life.

He always was curious and wanted to learn. He asked people a lot of questions and read a lot of magazines—*Life, Time, Consumer Reports, Popular Mechanics, National Geographic* and more. He was such a good role model for those who wanted to know more. I think he even read the encyclopedia.

Dad was always very supportive and encouraging especially when we had trouble in school, with boys, or didn't get the job we wanted. He loved to tell stories and make people laugh. He was really flattered when asked to talk about his World War II adventures at the Osher Lifelong Learning Institute. He had a very positive outlook on life that rubbed off on me.

The event that really made him my hero was when he was told he had to have his leg amputated to save his life. That was a very difficult decision for him. He would have to have an artificial leg to walk. He decided to have the operation, and he put up with tremendous pain as it healed. He had to go to two nursing homes to recover, as mom was unable to care for him. Gradually, he made peace with being at the nursing home, not being able to walk with the artificial leg, and being confined to the wheelchair. He could still talk to people, he still had a sharp mind, he could use CitiLift to go to the doctor's appointments, and the country club to meet with his buddies for lunch.

He left me with a lot of good examples to live up to, the value of a positive attitude, especially when things get you down, and a hero to remember every day of my life.

THEN · AGAIN

A DAY IN THE LIFE

- by Susan S.

Is childbirth an act of being brave? After all, you know something is coming when you decide to have a baby, but you never know what.

So as I prepared for the birth of my second child, I was filled with excitement and nervousness. I was now remarried to a wonderful man, and we were 2 years into our marriage and awaiting the birth of our child together. Both of us were geriatric parents—me at 36 and he at 41. My second child, his first—although he considered my son from my first marriage like his own.

The day started like most others in that late stage of pregnancy. The baby wasn't due for two weeks, but I was off work due to my blood pressure with orders to stay in bed except to go to the doctor.

This particular day was Ted's and my second wedding anniversary, and my oldest son was visiting his dad back in Illinois. Ted and I were living in Salem, Oregon where my job had taken us. We knew the baby would be coming soon and looked forward to this last meal out before the baby came.

Reservations had been made at The Inn at Orchard Heights for 7 pm. In those days the sex of the baby was a surprise. I slept in that day and then headed for the doctor in the afternoon. As I was being checked, the doctor said my blood pressure was too high, and I needed to have the baby soon. The doctor was going on vacation the next day, and since it was Friday, he made the decision to break my water in the doctor's office with the instruction that I was to go to the hospital when the labor started. He said I would have the baby between 10pm and midnight. Boy was he wrong!

After the nurse broke the water and was complaining about the mess she had to clean up, I headed for my car. Well that's when the labor started! The doctor was in West Salem which meant I had to cross the huge Willamette River and it was now rush hour. Oh my gosh! I don't think I can drive myself home in labor with contractions coming frequently. This is before cell phones—what am I going to do?

Mind you, when we moved to Salem, we only knew 3 other families that I worked with at the insurance company where I was employed. I decided to drive to Teresa and Jeff's house as I knew she was a nurse, and I'd be safe having her drive me home. Fortunately, they lived a few blocks from the doctor's office, but their house was up and down a series of huge hills. Jeff was mowing the yard, and I got out of the car holding my side. He ran up to me and asked what was wrong, and I announced that I was in labor! A scene from any sitcom ensued. Teresa came rushing out with a garbage bag to put on the seat of her car. Ted would have to get my car later.

As we headed over the bridge in rush hour, the contractions became stronger, but I breathed a sigh of relief that at least I didn't have the baby on the bridge. Teresa dropped me off at home. My bag was already packed as had been instructed in the prenatal classes. When I came in the house, Ted started complaining about his ankle which he had sprained—or was it his wrist—anyway, it was uncharacteristic for me to yell, "I don't care about that now. I'm having a baby".

Well the sitcom scenes started once again. We hopped in his pick-up truck as my car was now at the friend's house. It was just 10 minutes to the hospital, but boy was that a long 10 minutes and very bumpy in the truck as I was now in heavy labor.

Now we are at the hospital. I suppose it was 5:45pm by then. Of course the first thing they wanted was their $250 co-pay. I had to explain, and what this woman didn't understand, was that I was going to have a baby and SOON! She finally saw it my way and skipped the $250. She explained that it was Friday night and that the business office wouldn't be open for the weekend. I told her, "Trust me, you'll get your money, but not NOW," unless she planned on delivering the baby!

I am now in the birthing room with the nurses rapidly asking pertinent questions for their paperwork before I delivered. The nurse asked, "Have you taken any street drugs?"

My response: "No, but if you have some I'll give them a try." The nurse said it couldn't be that bad, or I wouldn't be joking around. She then told me that I would have to wait until the doctor got there as he was at a restaurant having his dinner.

I had to inform her that they'd better find someone else as I felt like pushing NOW! Well, Dr H. arrived in the knick of time to deliver Joseph Zachary S. at 7:10p.m. From hitting the West Salem bridge to delivery—1 hour 55 minutes.

They were probably just giving away our table at the restaurant.

MY FIRST HOME

- by Kenny Carrigan

My first home was in the south side of Peoria at 429 Hulbert Street. This is the house that I came home to when I was born in October of 1934. The population of the city of Peoria hasn't changed much over the years; however, most of us lived in the valley at that time in history.

The houses were so close together that I could stand and touch the side of our house and the side of the house next door at the same time. Now, this compactness lends itself to a great many houses being located in any one city block, with the exception of our block. Our block contained an industrial building, Peoria Apron & Towel Company, as well as the St. Joseph Catholic Church, School, Parsonage, and the living quarters of the Sisters who taught in the school.

We also had an additional unique item in that the Hulbert streetcar line ran right past the front of our house. The streetcars had lots of people riding on them, as none of us owned a car at that time. The streetcars were always well lighted at night as they received electricity to operate them from an overhead bare wire that was stretched high over the center of the two iron rails which the streetcars ran on. The iron rails were flush with the bricks in our street.

The conductor always utilized a universal signal of clanging a large bell which was located under the streetcar. This was a safety procedure to warn both the riders on the streetcar as well as those individuals that were pedestrians. It was always one LOUD clang to indicate an imminent stop; and two LOUD clangs to indicate that the car was about to start up and go forward. (They could not go in reverse without an extensive procedure).

I was always amazed when we had out-of-town guests stay overnight and would invariably say the next morning that they didn't get much sleep due to the noise from the streetcars running late into the night and then starting again early in the morning.

This amazed me because I never was awakened by them, or ever heard them for that matter. These were the sounds I had grown up with, which my subconscious mind had blocked out. I didn't get to ride on the streetcars very often as they were very expensive, three tokens for a dime, if I remember correctly.

My dad worked as a construction electrician, and he would take his lunch bucket and his tool box with him on the streetcar when he would leave for work in the mornings.

As I got older, the bigger kids taught me how to "Wrap a Trolley" which worked perfectly on my street. From my house there were about three blocks of straight tracks to the North and four blocks of tracks to the South, then a ninety degree turn at each end.

The streetcars were designed with a cowcatcher on both ends, which was perfect to jump up on at a stop, and to ride while hanging on for dear life. The cowcatchers were similar to the height of a bumper on a car. They differed from a car bumper in that they were about eighteen inches deep and they were constructed of plate steel. (My mother would have had a cow if she had seen me riding on one of these.)

Everything on the streetcars ran entirely on direct current electricity, the drive motors, and the electric heaters in the winter months, as well as the lighting. They received their electricity as a moving item by virtue of a collector going up from the rear of the cars. Now this electricity collector had a rope that ran from just below the collecting point of the arm down to a 12" spring-loaded reel that was attached to the back of every streetcar. The purpose was to allow a conductor to have a means of putting the collecting wheel back on the wire if it came off.

Here's the program: 1st Jump on a cowcatcher when a streetcar stopped to pick up or drop off a passenger. 2nd Hang low so that the conductor doesn't see you. 3rd Hang on by the elbow of your left arm while you pull some of the additional rope out of the spring-loaded reel and wrap it around the steel exterior of the rope reel. 4th Jump off at the next stop, and hide. Then 5th watch as the streetcar starts around the curve and looses all electricity as the collector comes off of the overhead wire. 6th listen as the conductor cusses you damn kids, saying he is going to call the police on us, as he is working un-wrapping the trolley rope and places the collector back on the wire.

Total damage to the streetcar—none! Total damage to the conductor's blood pressure—probably severe. Total down time for a streetcar from "wrapping"—3 to 5 minutes. Entertainment value to neighborhood kids—immense!

The police would check the area for a few days, and we would limit our activities for a couple of months, then we would "Wrap a Trolley" once again.

No, we never were caught!

MOM

by Carla Rich Montez

You let me wear your high heels when I played house.

My hair looked beautiful in my school pictures.

We baked cookies together.

You took me to church every Sunday.

I know you talked to my teachers when you suspected they were not being fair to me.

You picked out the white go-go boots that Santa gave me.

Piano lessons were twenty miles away, and you drove me there every week.

My sheets always smelled like they had just come in from the clothesline.

You attended every concert, contest, and softball game.

I learned about yoga watching you.

I never heard you swear – except when you hit your head.

Getting a gerbil *was* a bad idea.

I was allowed to play my records really loud.

You let me raise the orphaned baby raccoon.

I liked helping you in the garden.

Canning corn together was something I looked forward to every summer.

You played the piano for me when I sang at church.

I know you worried when I rode my bike on the hard road.

You were my favorite 4-H leader because you were so kind.

We played piano duets together and laughed to tears when we got out of sync.

I fed the baby lambs with a pop bottle full of warm milk.

You listened to me.

My lunch box always had frosted graham crackers in it.

You let me look at the Sears® catalog while you trimmed my bangs.

I know how much you loved me.

———————————

THEN · AGAIN

EPILOGUE

Finally, the conditions are perfect.

You've read some terrific examples of real life stories; you've written down a few of your own memories; and you have a ready audience of family and friends urging you to write. You have everything you need to write the story of your life.

So begin. Today. Write a couple of pages about the best friend you ever had or a time when you took a chance. And then write some more stories—about your parents and your summer vacation and your 21st birthday.

Relive your life—and write about it.

Go enjoy your Then, Again.

Section 3

FREQUENTLY ASKED QUESTIONS

After 20+ years of teaching life story writing, I have noticed that the same questions come up in nearly every class. Here are some of them, and my answers.

Who is the audience when I'm writing my life story? Who am I writing for?
The answer to this question changes as your writing develops. In the beginning, you will probably write for your children and grandchildren because you want the next generation to know what your life was like. Your family may also be asking you to document some of the stories you're known for telling

Later in your writing, you may discover that you're writing for yourself. As you revisit your past, you will gain some new perspective about your life. You'll see things differently. In this process, you may realize you are writing for the pleasure your writing brings to you.

What is the difference between a genealogy and a life story?
Both are activities that help us document our family history, but they are very different processes. In the genealogy, the goal is to determine a line of descent. This is typically accomplished by reviewing public records like birth and death certificates, marriage licenses, and similar documents that provide us factual details about ancestors.

Another way to convey our family history is to share our stories. When we can read the personal accounts of our predecessors' experiences, we gain insights about their state of mind. Unlike the evidence-based genealogy, the life story is more qualitative. It reveals the feelings and emotions that accompany the facts of our lives.

You described a story as a single event or memory. How long should one of those be?

It's easy to write too much, and this is why my assignments have a 2- or 3-page limit. This rule causes writers to be more concise with words and more selective about details. As a result, the stories are still complete, just less wordy.

I also remind my workshop members that Lincoln wrote the *Gettysburg Address* in only 272 words. Most would agree that its brevity did not compromise its message.

Some people are better writers than I am, so I'm reluctant to share my stories. Do you have any suggestions for me?

There is no "best" way or "right" way to express your own memories. You get to choose what you want to say and how you want to say it. After all, it's your life story, and no one can write it better than you. Besides, your writing is for your pleasure, not for anyone's approval.

But here's a tip if you're still concerned about your writing skills. Write like you talk, and then don't do much editing and fixing once you've written a story. You may discover that your writing will come more easily when you stop listening to the critic in your head. Furthermore, your family and friends will enjoy "hearing" you in your stories. It's a terrific accomplishment when your stories cause your readers to tell you, "That sounds just like you."

You spend a lot of time talking about the senses and how you can use them to connect to your memories. Aren't there other ways to remember?

If you visit any bookstore or website, you'll finds dozens of resources that will help trigger your memories. I encourage you to use any of them. But I still favor using my senses. The process of quieting my mind and paying attention has a good effect on both me and my writing. I've become more present and aware as a result.

I took your advice, and I asked some people to read my stories and give me some feedback. But I don't agree with some of their suggestions. What do I do now?
At one time or another in our lives, we've all asked for advice, and then wished we hadn't. When this advice applies to your writing, it can have a particular sting because it may feel like someone is trying to change your voice or rewrite your memories. So when you sense that your reviewer is overreaching, thoughtfully consider the advice, nod appreciatively, offer a few "I sees" and "uh huhs," and then do what you know is best. It's your story. You're the expert here.

But when your critic is spot on and offers a worthwhile suggestion, make the change.

What do I do with the bad memories?
I don't think we should ignore painful memories. They have lessons. But I also believe you should be careful about sharing stories that may be hurtful to others. Don't use your life story as an instrument for getting even or setting the record straight. Doing so will only make you look bitter and resentful, and that's not the legacy you want to leave. Instead, write about those bad memories, and then burn them. As you watch the smoke rise from the ashes, thank the bad memories for what they taught you, and then let them go.

But let me be clear about one thing. If your memories are so painful and so deep that they drain away all your joy and enthusiasm, get help. Talk with a counselor or a professional whose wisdom and kindness will guide you in a healing way.

I don't want to write a book. I just want to jot down a few of my favorite memories. What options are available for me?
Are you familiar with fill-in books? Typically, these books consist of questions or statements that help trigger memories, and then they allocate space where you can write your responses. For example, fill-in books might include prompts like these: "Describe the first house you lived in." "What do you remember about your favorite teacher?" "When you were in high school, what clubs did you join?" Not only are fill-in books great for capturing the highlights of your life, they are easy to complete. Plus they make wonderful gifts!

You have an interesting approach to life story writing. Would you mind if I used some of your ideas to lead my own life story writing workshop?
I am so pleased that you are inspired to teach! You are welcome to use any of my ideas to help you teach others how to write their life stories. And take a look at the section of this book that is designed for teachers. You might find some more ideas there.

Your book contains several life stories that were written by your workshop members. What can you tell us about them?
I am so honored to showcase the writing of some of my "students." Most of them are first-time life story writers just like you. They also just happen to have an average age of 70. Aren't their stories amazing?

How did you come up with the title for your book?
It's a play on words, but it fits. When you write your life story, you are reliving your past. Or to put it in the form of a book title, you're living then, again.

THEN · AGAIN

Section 4

IDEAS FOR TEACHERS

While this book is designed for people who want to write their life stories, it can also be a valuable resource if you are leading your own life story writing program. If you can use my materials to help even one person write his or her life story, you will have honored my work.

- Your writers will share deeply personal stories and feelings, so make your classroom a safe and enjoyable place for them. Show your participants that they will be heard, that they will not be judged, that their ideas are valued, and that their interactions will be held in confidence. In such a trustworthy environment, the work can be extraordinarily meaningful.

- Assign story topics. For example, ask participants to write about a holiday they remember, or their first grade teacher, or their memories about singing in the choir. These prompts serve two purposes.
  - o First, they help the student who can't come up with a story idea. They're memory joggers.
  - o Second, assignments imply that writing is expected—that you're not going to just talk about life story writing, you're going to do life story writing.

- Let them read. The bulk of your class time should be devoted to participants reading their stories aloud in class. Here's why:
  - o When they listen to each other's stories, your participants are exposed to different writing styles. This may lead to experimentation in their own writing.
  - o Memories are triggered when you listen to others' stories.
  - o When you read your own story aloud, you hear things you'd like to change. Your participants will edit their own writing when they can hear themselves.

- Let reading be optional for those group members who may be uncomfortable reading in front of a group, or for those who lack confidence in their writing. But talk to them privately about their decision. Remind them of the benefits of reading aloud, and encourage them to try. With your support, they will read when they feel comfortable.

- Set limits on story length. Two to three pages is the ideal length for a story. This has two benefits:
  o   A memory is typically quite easy to recount in two or three pages. Success is quick and effortless, and these both foster continued writing.
  o   By setting a page limit, you are helping writers who are inclined to be wordy. It compels them to make decisions about what to keep and what to leave out.

- Require feedback. Feedback is an essential component of writing. It improves writing, and it reminds us that writing is not done in isolation. Feedback is also an indicator of genuine concern of one writer for another. We help each other.

- Model appropriate feedback. As the leader of the group, provide verbal feedback after each participant reads his or her story aloud. Through your example, your participants will learn what is expected when it's their turn to offer feedback.

- When feedback is expected of every member, you are also developing their critical listening skills.

- Eventually, pair group members, and invite them to work together outside of class. Such teamwork fosters collaboration and encourages creativity.

- Use grammar and usage errors as teachable moments. When you observe that there is widespread confusion about a grammar rule, for example, the usage of it's vs its, take the opportunity to conduct a brief refresher. While grammar should not be the focus of your program, its review is helpful—and often appreciated—when you see errors that are consistent among your participants.

• Invite reflection. During the last ten minutes of your workshop, pose an engaging question, and ask your students to respond to it, in writing, in a special notebook that you collect at the end of class. "What did you think about today's stories?" "Why does writing matter to you?" Prompts like these guide writers to think more deeply about the class and their own writing, and this process often leads to new insights for them.

Reading these reflections also guides me. Sometimes participants' comments show me how they are processing the work. This feedback helps me identify where I need to fill gaps in their learning.

• Practice presence. Begin each class by giving your students a moment to collect their thoughts—to get them in their "writing minds." Ask them to look out the window and study the view. Invite them to close their eyes and still their thoughts. Engage them in some brief yoga poses or in a labyrinth walk. In other words, help your students clear their minds for writing. As they practice being present, your writers will also learn that it helps them pay attention, which is the most important skill a writer can have.

• Reminiscing can be an emotional experience especially when a memory is sentimental. So bring a box of tissues to every class, and make sure your writers know there is no shame in expressing their feelings.

• Life story writing can be therapeutic, but unless you're a professional counselor, therapy is not your work. If you experience situations that require knowledge beyond your expertise, refer your participants to a clinician.

• Offer a break. Aside from the necessary bathroom visit, the break gives participants an opportunity to move their bodies, to chat with each other, and to enjoy any snacks that may be available. Breaks rejuvenate us for further writing.

- Because nature inspires writing, I encourage you to hold your writing program in a location where windows will allow a clear view of the outdoors. A natural setting also allows you to extend your classroom outside where you can ask your group members to look for memories through sensory observations they make in the natural world.

- At the end of every course, I ask students to submit their stories for inclusion in a class book which each of them will receive. I have been told many times that this book is a valued component of the course and that it is frequently re-read after the class has ended.

- To ensure that the book will be attractive when it's duplicated, I ask my participants to follow some basic formatting guidelines. These include suggestions about fonts, spacing, and margins, but also cover recommendations to write on only one side of the paper and to include their names at the top of every page.

- I have found that the optimal size for a workshop is 15 people. This class size ensures that each person will have several opportunities to read over the course of my 6-week program.

- My classes meet every other week. This scheduling gives the students ample time to write their stories and sufficient time for me to review and comment on them between sessions.

- I run a low-tech class which means I use very little audio-visual equipment, and I require my participants to silence their cell phones during class. I take this stance for two reasons. First, a low-tech classroom offers participants a short reprieve from their technology-rich lives. Second, we can sometimes attend to each other better when technology is removed from the experience.

- Don't be discouraged if the writing in your class develops to a point where your members outgrow the class. As their writing skills mature, they may elect to explore new writing groups and experiences. Encourage this growth in your writers.

- Conduct course evaluations. Participant feedback is good for you and your program.

- Make stories part of the record. With your participants' permission, contact a librarian, and ask that your students' stories be catalogued into the library's collection. Fifty years from now, someone will be grateful that they found a story written by their great-great-grandfather because your library archived it and made it accessible on the Internet.

- Consider offering an annual life story writing retreat in a location away from your home base. The opportunity to "run away and write" facilitates uninterrupted writing and encourages the development of community among your participants.

ABOUT THE AUTHOR

Carla Rich Montez

Carla Rich Montez was first recognized as a writer when her 1-page theme paper was published in the newsletter of the county superintendent of schools. She was ten. Since then, Carla has involved herself in every kind of writing: from news stories to features; from ad copy to website copy; from script writing to magazine writing. Along the way, she has also composed trail guides, travel guides, and instructional materials, has carried out dozens of freelance projects, and has written or edited hundreds of brochures and publicity pieces.

In her 40s, Carla's writing experiences positioned her to be recruited to co-teach life story writing workshops in a growing university-based lifelong learning program for retirees. Eventually, she developed and led its life story writing program which, for the next twenty years, helped hundreds of participants write their own life stories.

Today, Carla lives in Central Illinois where she continues to write and teach while enjoying her three amazing children, her loving husband, and her devoted dogs. In her free time, she regularly hikes, kayaks, and practices yoga.

Then · Again is Carla's first book.

www.ingramcontent.com/pod-product-compliance
Lightning Source LLC
LaVergne TN
LVHW011219080426
835509LV00005B/212